DIY: The Search for Control and Self-Reliance in the 21st Century

Kevin Wehr

From the driveway mechanic to the backyard gardener, many diverse people are "doing it themselves" by building or repairing the stuff of their daily lives without the aid of experts. *DIY* uses Habermas's colonization of the lifeworld as a frame and mobilizes Marx's concepts of alienation and mystification to examine how social behaviors can be a conscious reply to a complex and fast-moving world, a nostalgia for simpler times past, or just an economic impulse. Each main chapter is anchored by an extended empirical example: back to the land, home schooling, and self-government.

Kevin Wehr is Associate Professor of Sociology at California State University, Sacramento, where he specializes in environmental, political, and cultural sociology. He received his PhD in 2002 and his MS in 1998 from the University of Wisconsin, Madison, and his BA in 1994 from the University of California, Santa Cruz. His other works include *America's Fight over Water: The Environmental and Political Effects of Large-Scale Water Systems* and *Hermes on Two Wheels: The Sociology of Bicycle Messengers.*

 University Readers
Reading Materials Evolved.

 THE SOCIAL ISSUES COLLECTION™

 Routledge
Taylor & Francis Group

Framing 21st Century Social Issues

The goal of this new, unique Series is to offer readable, teachable "thinking frames" on today's social problems and social issues by leading scholars. These are available for view on http://routledge.customgateway.com/routledge-social-issues.html.

For instructors teaching a wide range of courses in the social sciences, the Routledge *Social Issues Collection* now offers the best of both worlds: originally written short texts that provide "overviews" to important social issues *as well as* teachable excerpts from larger works previously published by Routledge and other presses.

As an instructor, click to the website to view the library and decide how to build your custom anthology and which thinking frames to assign. Students can choose to receive the assigned materials in print and/or electronic formats at an affordable price.

Available

Body Problems
Running and Living Long in a Fast-Food Society
Ben Agger

Sex, Drugs, and Death
Addressing Youth Problems in American Society
Tammy Anderson

The Stupidity Epidemic
Worrying About Students, Schools, and America's Future
Joel Best

Empire Versus Democracy
The Triumph of Corporate and Military Power
Carl Boggs

Contentious Identities
Ethnic, Religious, and Nationalist Conflicts in Today's World
Daniel Chirot

The Future of Higher Education
Dan Clawson and Max Page

Waste and Consumption
Capitalism, the Environment, and the Life of Things
Simonetta Falasca-Zamponi

Rapid Climate Change
Causes, Consequences, and Solutions
Scott G. McNall

The Problem of Emotions in Societies
Jonathan H. Turner

Outsourcing the Womb
Race, Class, and Gestational Surrogacy in a Global Market
France Winddance Twine

Changing Times for Black Professionals
Adia Harvey Wingfield

DIY: The Search for Control and Self-Reliance in the 21st Century

Kevin Wehr

California State University, Sacramento

Routledge
Taylor & Francis Group

NEW YORK AND LONDON

First published 2012
by Routledge
711 Third Avenue, New York, NY 10017

Simultaneously published in the UK
by Routledge
2 Park Square, Milton Park, Abingdon, Oxon OX14 4RN

Routledge is an imprint of the Taylor & Francis Group, an informa business

© 2012 Taylor & Francis

Library of Congress Cataloging in Publication Data
Wehr, Kevin.
DIY : the search for control and self-reliance in the 21st century / Kevin Wehr. —
1st ed.
p. cm. — (Framing 21st century social issues)
Includes bibliographical references and index.
1. Interpersonal relations. 2. Do-it-yourself work. 3. Self-reliant living.
I. Title. II. Title: Doing it yourselves.
HM1106.W44 2012
179'.9—dc23
2012004171

ISBN13: 978-0-415-50871-1 (pbk)
ISBN13: 978-0-203-12528-1 (ebk)

Typeset in Garamond and Gill Sans
by EvS Communication Networx, Inc.

University Readers (www.universityreaders.com): Since 1992, University
Readers has been a leading custom publishing service, providing reasonably priced,
copyright-cleared course packs, custom textbooks, and custom publishing services
in print and digital formats to thousands of professors nationwide. The Routledge
Custom Gateway provides easy access to thousands of readings from hundreds of
books and articles via an online library. The partnership of University Readers and
Routledge brings custom publishing expertise and deep academic content together
to help professors create perfect course materials that are affordable to students.

Printed and bound in the United States of America by Publishers Graphics,
LLC on sustainably sourced paper.

Contents

Series Foreword

The world in the early 21st century is beset with problems—a troubled economy, global warming, oil spills, religious and national conflict, poverty, HIV, health problems associated with sedentary lifestyles. Virtually no nation is exempt, and everyone, even in affluent countries, feels the impact of these global issues.

Since its inception in the 19th century, sociology has been the academic discipline dedicated to analyzing social problems. It is still so today. Sociologists offer not only diagnoses; they glimpse solutions, which they then offer to policy makers and citizens who work for a better world. Sociology played a major role in the civil rights movement during the 1960s in helping us to understand racial inequalities and prejudice, and it can play a major role today as we grapple with old and new issues.

This series builds on the giants of sociology, such as Weber, Durkheim, Marx, Parsons, Mills. It uses their frames, and newer ones, to focus on particular issues of contemporary concern. These books are about the nuts and bolts of social problems, but they are equally about the frames through which we analyze these problems. It is clear by now that there is no single correct way to view the world, but only paradigms, models, which function as lenses through which we peer. For example, in analyzing oil spills and environmental pollution, we can use a frame that views such outcomes as unfortunate results of a reasonable effort to harvest fossil fuels. "Drill, baby, drill" sometimes involves certain costs as pipelines rupture and oil spews forth. Or we could analyze these environmental crises as inevitable outcomes of our effort to dominate nature in the interest of profit. The first frame would solve oil spills with better environmental protection measures and clean-ups, while the second frame would attempt to prevent them altogether, perhaps shifting away from the use of petroleum and natural gas and toward alternative energies that are "green."

These books introduce various frames such as these for viewing social problems. They also highlight debates between social scientists who frame problems differently. The books suggest solutions, both on the macro and micro levels. That is, they suggest what new policies might entail, and they also identify ways in which people, from the ground level, can work toward a better world, changing themselves and their lives and families and providing models of change for others.

Readers do not need an extensive background in academic sociology to benefit from these books. Each book is student-friendly in that we provide glossaries of terms for the uninitiated that are keyed to bolded terms in the text. Each chapter ends with questions for further thought and discussion. The level of each book is accessible to undergraduate students, even as these books offer sophisticated and innovative analyses.

In his book, Kevin Wehr addresses an intriguing new movement in America, involving self-help. From the driveway mechanic to the backyard gardener, many diverse people are "doing it themselves" by building or repairing the stuff of their daily lives without the aid of experts. His book on do-it-yourselfers uses Habermas's colonization of the lifeworld as a frame and mobilizes Marx's concepts of alienation and mystification to examine how social behaviors can be a conscious reply to a complex and fast-moving world, a nostalgia for simpler times past, or just an economic impulse. Each of his chapters is anchored by an extended empirical example involving back to the land, home schooling, and self-government. His is a fascinating foray into what happens "off the grid" of official sociology and social life.

Preface
Why DIY?

What does it mean to do it yourself (DIY)? While it may seem flippant, this is actually a non-trivial question. There is a broad range of human behaviors that could qualify as DIY. From the driveway mechanic to the backyard gardener or the home-schooling parents, many diverse people are "doing it themselves." There are also people who have made a conscious decision to lead a life out of the mainstream: workers who band together into a cooperative, or punks living in collectively governed urban "squats," or hippies who move "back to the land." DIY is both varied in character and broad in scope. But at its core is a simple idea: the tasks that many are ready and willing to have others do for them can (and perhaps should) be done by one's self.

DIY at its most basic means that ordinary people build or repair the stuff of their daily lives without the aid of experts. This could be a home improvement project, posting a YouTube video, or building a bicycle—perhaps you consult a guidebook, but the project is done independently. DIY can be bigger than the home though. DIY endeavors also include running a pirate radio station, publishing your own blog or magazine (known as a "'zine"), or even creating your own record label.

Why study the do-it-yourself movement? One simple reason is that people across the nation engage in DIY behaviors on a daily basis, intentionally or not. This might be reason enough, but it masks a deeper reality that many "do-it-yourselfers" live in. DIY can be a conscious reply to a complex and fast-moving world. It can be a politicized response to the proliferation of technology that seems to rule our lives—some DIYers are like modern-day Luddites who resist the lure of the machine. It can also be a non-political reflex, akin to the phrase "if you want something done right, do it yourself," or it might be motivated out of a nostalgia for simpler times past. And of course some DIYers do it simply to save money. Sociology, as a framework for understanding society, can help make sense of behaviors that might seem irrational or inefficient on the surface (why preserve your own food when you can just buy it year round in the store?)—behaviors that actually have internal logic once you dig more deeply.

Sociology, as an academic discipline, also has a goal of understanding human behaviors in all their manifestations. DIY is hardly a social movement on the order of the civil rights or student movements past. But the collective behavior of multitudes of people in a particular direction certainly deserves notice. This book will attempt to understand the variety of DIY action—both socially organized action and individuals in their daily lives acting without broader coordination.

On a more personal level, I must declare that I am an avid do-it-yourselfer. I grow organic food in my backyard, then cook and preserve it in the kitchen. I built the coop for my chickens, and I repair my car and house to the extent of my abilities. Why am I this way? Partly it is a result of early-childhood socialization: I was raised in a family where weekends were spent doing chores around the house, where we cooked our own meals every day, and I was responsible for doing my own laundry as soon as I could see over the top of the washing machine. But on a deeper level, I have come to understand the value—both practical and theoretical—of knowing how things work and how to repair them. There is a form of demystification involved in my commitment to DIY. I feel that if I know how things work, I have more control in a world that can feel increasingly unmanageable.

And this is another motivation for many DIYers: it is gratifying to be able to do it without the help of experts. Ralph Waldo Emerson wrote about self-reliance in the middle of the 19th century and noted that it was a peculiarly American trait. But in the last 150 years, self-reliance has diminished dramatically. Perhaps this, too, is one reason why being self-sufficient feels good to many in the DIY movement: doing it yourself feels like a lost art and a preservation of esoteric knowledge, especially in our time when technologies drive so much of the world around us—technologies that most of us don't fully understand. In fact, there is an identity-construction process around some of these activities: people may start out as just another beer drinker but end up as a home brewer. Many DIYers come to label themselves in interesting and novel ways, which is yet another reason to examine them as a social group.

This book has five chapters. The first outlines the types of DIY people and groups, and examines DIY behavior from a broader theoretical view. Each subsequent chapter uses the theoretical foundation developed in Chapter I to examine specific groupings of DIY activities, with each chapter anchored by a key empirical example: back-to-the-landers in Chapter II, home-schoolers in Chapter III, and self-government in Chapter IV. Chapter V offers concluding thoughts.

Perhaps this book will help you to see your actions in a new way. It might open your eyes to a world where you can do more than you thought. Most of us can. Perhaps more of us should.

I would like to thank the editors and anonymous reviewers for keen insights that helped improve the book. I'd also like to thank my DIY reading group, Loran and Evan, for illuminating discussions on these issues. I dedicate this book to Ellen, my partner in DIY life.

1:   A Good Idea, in Theory

❧

I walk into the library downtown. It is an unseasonably warm but otherwise normal day here, with students from an elementary school gathered in the children's section, unemployed folks looking to improve their skill-set reading computer software manuals, and a homeless man attempting to clean up a bit in the restroom. I run a computer search on "do it yourself" and come up with thousands of entries. I wander into the stacks. The number of titles is overwhelming: *The Complete Fix-it Manual*, *Lawn Care for Dummies*, *The Whole Earth Catalog*, and even *How to Eat*. There are guides to fixing your car, landscaping your yard, and improving communication with your spouse. A similar search for "self-help" turns up an even larger number of titles. What is going on here? Why are so many people writing books about how to help people help themselves?

Doing it yourself seems like a good idea, in theory. It also sounds like hard work. Sometimes it is work, but DIYers often find this work to be rewarding in ways that make it worthwhile. To some it might feel a waste of time to grow and preserve your own food, or educate your children at home. It seems an inefficient duplication of effort—after all there is well-preserved food to be bought at the grocery store, and we all pay taxes to support the public schools whether we use them or not. So why do DIYers bother? Before exploring detailed examples of **DIY**, we must situate the concept in its social and theoretical context and try to understand "why" on a broad level.

The term Do It Yourself includes many varied people and groups. The simplest definition is when ordinary people build or repair the things in their daily lives without the aid of experts. This could be working on the house, growing food in the backyard, or fixing the car. Do-it-yourselfers might consult a manual or self-help book, but in order to be truly DIY, the project must be done independently of professionals. DIY includes more than home improvement chores, though. DIY endeavors could also include larger local projects like running a **pirate radio** station, publishing a magazine from your own desktop, creating an independent music recording label, or participating in a regional alternative economy like Ithaca, New York's "Ithaca hours" where people volunteer for community service and get credit to spend with local businesses in return.

Some DIYers volunteer while others get paid, so it is important to differentiate between being DIY and being entrepreneurial. Starting your own non-profit record label in order to regain control from the music industry is one thing, but doing so because you want to make money is more complicated. DIY in general does not mean being entrepreneurial, but making a few bucks off it does not necessarily contradict the logic.

In short, DIY means people are taking control of their lives, becoming more **self-reliant**. Almost 170 years ago, the transcendentalist philosopher Ralph Waldo Emerson wrote his famous essay "Self-Reliance" (2010 [1841]). Emerson's essay is a meditation on an individual's place within society as well as the virtue of relying on one's self. Emerson argued that we should reject rules that diminish liberty:

> Society is a joint-stock company, in which the members agree for the better securing of his bread to each shareholder, to surrender the liberty and culture of the eater.
>
> (19)

Emerson regretted the lack of self-reliance among men (he means all people, not just males) and our dependence instead on experts: "I am ashamed to think how easily we capitulate to badges and names, to large societies and dead institutions" (19).

Emerson wanted us to be free of control by professionals: "It is easy to see that a greater self-reliance … must work a revolution in all the offices and relations of men" (37). In many ways this is a philosophical foundation for doing it yourself. Emerson called on Americans to free themselves of reliance on social institutions and discover our own motivations within. In short: do your own thing. Since Emerson, DIY in the United States has a long history with diverse examples and offshoots.

The do-it-yourself movement offers an interesting chance to analyze quite disparate people and groups. There are punks, hippies, and good ol' boys. There are backyard gardeners, home-schoolers, and bike messengers. Many of these folks would cringe to find themselves in a category together, but they share a common thread that we might draw through the analysis to help us understand our broader society a little more clearly.

There are at least three ways to situate the DIY movement, and do-it-yourselfers (DIYers). First, we can understand DIYers as individuals acting on their own inclinations. But there are also folks who embrace a DIY mentality and actively share this with others. If we call the first group **DIY individualists**, the second might be called **DIY coordinators**. Lastly, there are people entirely caught up in the idea of DIY, and follow it almost like a philosophy. They live a lifestyle devoted to the idea, so we might call them **DIY lifestylers**.

Individualists

Many DIYers are acting as individuals in isolation. They grow food for personal reasons—it makes them happy, or they find the produce to be of higher quality. Maybe

Figure 1.1 Do-it-yourself painting.
Source: Shutterstock

they do it to save money. As often happens when we focus only on individuals and think of DIYers as people simply acting on their own, we miss interesting things about the social context within which they act. Individualists may not think of themselves as a DIY type of person, or as engaging in DIY behavior. They may instead think of woodworking, painting, or knitting as simply a hobby. But even if they do not coordinate with other DIYers these folks are part of our larger society and rely on the coordination of the **market** for their weekend chores or hobbies. Most backyard gardeners would be lost without the nursery down the street to sell fertilizer and seeds. Without the auto parts store, the driveway mechanic couldn't buy the fan-belt she wants to install. Thus, DIYers are enmeshed in the larger capitalist system, even if they desire to break away from paying professionals. Reliance on others, then, is a continuum—from paying someone to do it, to buying a "do-it-yourself kit," to following detailed step-by-step instructions. Guidebooks provide assistance, but this can lessen the purity of a DIY endeavor. This can verge towards a "DIY-lite" where a project is done in a "color-by-numbers" manner. They are doing it themselves, but with a lot of help from distant experts.

Coordinators

The people who consciously embrace a DIY mentality and coordinate with a larger group are the core of what might be called the DIY movement. Perhaps they subscribe to *Readymade* magazine, follow a **blog** about their favorite DIY topics, or watch the DIY network on cable. They think about the DIY approach, and engage in DIY behaviors intentionally. Doing things themselves is a large part of who they are: they are DIY and proud of it.

Lifestylers

Beyond taking on the DIY label, there are those who live and breathe the DIY life-style. They believe in the philosophy, and their first reaction to a problem is "how can I fix this myself?" This is when DIY becomes political: lifestylers might make a major purchase (a car or a home) because they can fix it themselves, rather than choose one that is only able to be repaired by experts. They might take their DIY message to others through writing a blog or a **'zine**, and they think others should act more like them. They may reject products, situations, or even people because they do not conform to the DIY perspective. And most importantly, they devote a serious amount of time to their projects. These people are not the average weekend mechanic or gardener. As well as growing an extensive vegetable garden and home schooling their kids, they might keep bees or brew their own beer—processes that require time, commitment, and continued attention.

People who self-consciously live a DIY lifestyle might come from diverse points in our society. They might be punks who live outside the normal property-ownership system in an anarchist **squat**. They might be hippies who move to a collective farm. Or they might be from the culture of "good ol' boys" who together build a hunting camp. The commonality between these very different groups is that they see themselves as different from the larger surrounding society because they are committed to more extreme and intensive projects on their own rather than relying on experts.

So do the individualists, coordinators, and lifestylers make up a DIY social movement? Not in the classic sense of a group of like-minded people gathered together for the common purpose of bringing about change. Traditional social movements around issues like feminism or environmentalism have specific goals, strategies to achieve those goals, and a self-consciously political attitude. Most participants in the DIY movement, however, do not share a common goal or engage in concerted action. Instead they fall under Herbert Blumer's notion of "expressive action." In contrast to instrumental social movements, collective expressive behavior does not seek broad social change, but rather offers personal fulfillment for members (Blumer 1969). Examples include a knitting group or a 12-step program: The "individualists" or "coordinators" fall into this category. Lifestylers, on the other hand, might fit into the more traditional notion of a social movement. Because of the diversity of DIY action, there is no easy analytical model. What is certain is that people are doing it themselves across the United States, some in an inchoate manner, others acting together with common purpose. Some are just living their lives, others are self-consciously out to change the system.

Some examples of DIY shade into the notion of self-help. Self-help groups have some overlap with DIY: people are gathering together to seek assistance from each other without the aid of experts. But a distinction must be made. DIY involves a range of activities from changing your car's oil to running an interactive blog. These are the things of daily life, from home to food to school. Self-help on the other hand generally involves self-improvement and advocacy, such as what Alcoholics Anonymous or the National Association for the Mentally Ill offers. It is hard to imagine a support group for people who change their own oil. In general, DIY is not so much about self-improvement as about doing your own thing.

For the majority of society, a little DIY is cool, but a lot of DIY might seem strange. Brewing your own beer: cool. Composting your own feces to fertilize your garden: maybe not so cool. And there are those critics of DIY who argue that it is not only uncool, but a waste of time: "do-it-badly-yourself." There is a continuum of DIY behaviors and commitment. Working on your own home doesn't take a lot of commitment, and a lot of people engage in such DIY action. But with an increase in commitment to more extreme DIY projects, there is a drop-off in participation. What makes some elements of DIY invisible, others cool, and still others extreme? With the above typology in place, we can begin examining the broader social context that DIYers operate within.

Socialization is how we learn the rules of society: don't chew with your mouth open, always excuse yourself when you sneeze. We learn these rules from our family, school, church, peer groups, and from television. These primary socialization institutions help keep us in social conformity. Aggregating these behaviors, larger social institutions structure our actions, even if they seem invisible. Social institutions define the unwritten rules that govern our actions, ideals, goals, and in some ways our thoughts. In a capitalist economy, for instance, competition and risk are rewarded. People are taught these values in the marketplace, in school, and on the athletic field. Many consider them natural, but they aren't at all—they are learned social behaviors. The economy is one such social institution; there is also the family and the political realm, to highlight a few important examples. In our daily actions we produce and reproduce social institutions: we shop, vote, eat dinner, and life moves along.

Depending upon your view of a social institution, you may have a strong response, or you might not notice it at all. Millions of children are happily sent off to public schools each weekday. But some families are suspicious of the public schools, and have turned to teaching their kids at home. Similarly disenchanted with the corporate music business, some bands strike out on their own to produce music themselves. DIY can be a response (either intentional or unconscious) to the straightjacket character of many social institutions.

And so social institutions are reproduced (or not) and socialization continues on its track (or not) depending on the collected actions of millions of individuals. As individuals change their activities, social institutions and norms change slowly over time. For example, we live within social structures of racism and patriarchy as well as democracy and **capitalism**. These arrangements are quite stable, but they can change slowly over time due to social movements. All of us seek security, stability, and fulfillment, sometimes by making use of social structures, and sometimes by pushing against them. In our everyday actions we help to create and recreate those social structures—when we go to work, when we buy our groceries, when we pay our rent. Such mundane actions help to reproduce social structures, which then exert great power over individual behavior, both enabling certain freedoms, but also constraining many activities and ideas. DIY in our daily lives both reproduces and challenges social norms and institutions. DIY behavior is just as socially constructed as non-DIY behavior, though it may feel to some practitioners that they are challenging the status quo. In fact we can also see hierarchies in DIY, where lifestylers may look down on individualists for not being "DIY-enough." Of course, all DIY behavior is locked within the confines of what is possible within our society, and none of us can fully escape. Even Thoreau went home on occasion to do laundry and enjoy his mother's cooking. And DIY lifestylers often buy tools and supplies at the store, thus reproducing capitalism. We must understand DIY behavior as both reproducing and challenging social institutions and behavioral norms.

Why now? Why is DIY an up-and-coming issue of the 21st century? As will be discussed in Chapter II, people moved "**back to the land**" in several waves over the 20th century—what makes people doing the same thing now different? In some ways, not much. But in other ways the differences are significant. The philosophy of DIY helps to navigate the vagaries of modern life. For some, DIY becomes a way of life, a sense of community, and an identity that we attach to. More than 150 years ago, Karl Marx commented on how newer forms of the labor process produced isolation and detachment among workers, and described both **alienation** and **mystification** (1967 [1867]). Marx noticed that it seemed like people were missing something in their lives—there is a gap to be filled between our everyday experience and what we hope for.

For Marx, alienation and mystification were products of capitalism. Under a wage–labor system people are paid to produce a commodity. On an assembly line many workers make small additions to the overall production process, resulting in a product sold on the market. The worker walks away with a wage, and the capitalist who directs the process earns profit by selling the commodity. We are taught that this is fair and just: the capitalist buys machinery and raw materials up front and manages the overall process. Her profits are payment for the risk of investing. The laborers are simply paid a wage that is pegged to the prevailing market rate.

What Marx noticed about this was that the worker became separated from her labor in this process. Before factory production, a worker might make an individual item and sell it herself. The buyer knew who made the commodity, and the worker could take pride in the quality of what she produced. This is lost under capitalism, as most consumers have no idea who made a product, or how. This is alienation: the worker puts her time and energy—her very life force—into the commodity, which is then sold anonymously. For Marx this was a problem because it leaves a hole in the laborer's life, a lack of fulfillment. Many of us feel this too—who amongst us is totally fulfilled by our job? Alienation, for Marx, means a daily frustration at being detached from other workers and consumers. Social relationships of the past—where producers were united with consumers—have been replaced by wages and purchase prices: money now mediates the social relationship. Many DIYers seek to remove this mediation of social relationships and return to a system where people interact directly. As one DIY food enthusiast in San Francisco said, DIY is a resistance movement against the "corporate-run, food vendor governance board that says people cannot sell homemade dishes in a public venue without a license" (Pallo 2011).

Detachment from social relationships also produces mystification: the origins of goods we consume remain obscure to us. Most people today have no real knowledge of how the things they use on a daily basis actually work. The computer that I type on, the text messages I send, the update to my Facebook profile—none of these things do I understand on the fundamental basis of software codes and circuit boards. Most people don't even know truly how their car works. They simply take it to the mechanic when it stops (or worse, when it doesn't stop). From the electricity that lights our houses and powers our gadgets, to the water that flows from our taps, to where our waste goes when we flush the toilet—we live a life of blissful ignorance. All of these are products of the system, and remain mysterious to most of us. Many people who

Figure 1.2 Many drivers are mystified by the complexity of a car engine.
Source: Shutterstock

like to do it themselves notice these dual processes of alienation and mystification and make an attempt to solve the lack of fulfillment by learning how things work and doing the labor themselves. In other words, they want to put social relationships back into primacy over money or other abstractions, in an attempt to combat the sense of loss in our modern world. As one squat housing activist said: "Kids with no family created family here. We rehabbed the building, and the building rehabbed us" (Ferguson 2002). These DIYers are putting social relationships first, and learning how to rehabilitate their home and themselves.

Jurgen Habermas, a contemporary German social theorist, has a term for the ways that capitalism takes over social relationships, such as inserting money between producer and consumer: the **colonization of the lifeworld**. Habermas argues that our social lives can be understood as involving two different worlds: there is the world of economic production and politics (which he calls "**system**"), and the world of home, play, and sexual reproduction (which he calls "**lifeworld**"). *System* is characterized by bureaucracy, rationality, and instrumental means–ends calculations. *Lifeworld*, on the other hand, is characterized by shared values, norms based in morals or traditions, and personal relationships. Of course these two realms are not completely separate, for example intimate relationships are regulated by the government (marriage, domestic partnerships, divorce, alimony, etc.). Habermas calls this the "colonization of the lifeworld." The forces of capitalism and government insert themselves into our daily lives beyond the workplace: we buy things on the market (gasoline, groceries, clothes), and our private behaviors are governed (federally mandated health insurance, homosexuals cannot marry in most states). Money and power are the currency of the system, and wherever we see them in our daily lives it is likely that colonization has occurred. But, as with many processes, the colonization of the lifeworld has its reverse: decolonization. A guerilla gardener from Detroit illustrates Habermas's ideas clearly: "This is a way of decolonizing ourselves from the corporate food structure and doing something better at the same time" (Lee and Abowd 2011). Community gardens on vacant lots allow neighbors to resist the invasion of money and power into the farmer–consumer relationship.

The **decolonization of the lifeworld** comes as a result of politicized responses to the state or market—people come together to demand that the state reform racist, sexist, or homophobic policy. Of course these demands can also be coopted and recolonized in new ways (a process discussed later). To the extent we can collect the varieties of do-it-yourself action into a social movement, DIY is an attempt to decolonize the lifeworld.

But the system does not sit by and allow decolonization to proceed unchecked. Governments and capitalists put up barriers to DIYers all the time. Building codes are certainly an important part of modern life; without them we would be much less safe. But they also keep people from building their own house, or even fixing it up. Code enforcement necessitates the use of professionals and functions to keep contractors employed. The licensing of those contractors helps keep them up to date on government codes, but it also requires a separate bureaucracy. Barriers to DIY can be understood as a response to decolonization—they keep the government in control and capital making money. Money and power are at stake, and the result is that people are kept from doing things for themselves.

In this sense, DIY is a "take back." Instead of relying on experts, or the market, or the state, DIYers take back the personal matters of their lives from capitalism and bureaucracy. Many examples of this process will be the subject of the coming chapters, but one instance might suffice to illustrate the point. Long ago music took two forms: it was either composed by experts and commissioned by patrons, or created by normal people. The former is now generally known as "classical" music, while the latter is called "folk." Music made by folks is, of course, DIY. But folk music can take many forms: what once was a guy with a banjo singing ballads now can be a hip-hop rhymer. Folk music is just music made by and for "the folks," not a genre in-and-of-itself. But if you go into a music store, you will see categories of "folk," "rock," and "hip-hop." This is capitalism colonizing the lifeworld: the music made by folks is coopted into a mass-produced commodity, categorized, standardized, and sold back to "the folks." What do people do in response? They rebel in hundreds of creative ways. They trade free MP3 files on the Internet or start an independent record label. Artists cross genres or give music away for free. These are some of the most interesting and creative responses to governing social institutions.

But many of us much of the time are simply overwhelmed by forces that seem out of our control. Many people feel as if something new and different is going on, something that involves a loss of tradition and authentic identity or a diminution of culture. This sometimes takes the form of a collective nostalgia. We might feel that things were simpler in days gone by, and we yearn for less complexity and more control. Yet most of us certainly wouldn't want to give up our mobile phones, Internet, or cable TV. Nonetheless, there are strong forces within us that make us re-imagine history through a nostalgic lens. Whether it is Paris Hilton on *The Simple Life* or the imagined ideal community of the film *Pleasantville*, nostalgia for another time when things were less chaotic has a seductive hold on us. DIY is a response to this: DIYers take pride and pleasure in doing things the old way, the slow way, the way our grandparents did it.

Many of us feel a lack of control within the accelerated pace of life, which produces swirling identities and shifting meanings, causing many to crave stronger roots, a feeling of belonging, or an expression of solidarity. The search for control and rootedness is seen in real estate trends like "new urbanism," with neighborhoods that are more conducive to community building than the suburbs where most Americans currently live. The search for "realness" is manifested in the advertising world's "coolseekers," who comb the streets of Brooklyn or San Francisco for the next hip urban fad, to be mass-marketed to those of us who don't live in a cultural capital. We see it in the drive towards "extreme sports," where people push the envelope in search of exhilaration to offset the drudgery of an office job in a cubicle. Finding one's niche has often been a struggle, and contemporary society is no exception. In fact, technological change offers those who wander the Internet and the blogosphere new modes of identity to try out. New forms of community are multiplying, and some people are overwhelmed and paralyzed by the array.

When faced with such a wide variety of choices, it is easy to fall prey to a naive relativism, where any culture is available for cooptation or mimicry, and any choice seems as valid as any other. Today we can access 24-hour news and information from around the world brought to us by any one of thousands of websites. Commodities are assembled from parts crafted in sweatshop factories in several different nations of the **Global South**, then marketed and sold to first-world consumers at premium prices. Every television channel seems to report the same celebrity spectacle in mind-numbing minutiae, but news that really connects to our everyday lives is hard to come by.

In response, we get bloggers and independent media activists who purport to offer us "real" news or "on the ground" information. We see the rise of "handcrafted" products in place of homogenous plasticized trinkets. People move from identical houses in the suburbs to the gentrified city core, or to planned developments whose marketing references some lost, imaginary "Leave it to Beaver" time when community was more prevalent. This searching suggests a suspicion about the "official version" and a craving for authenticity. Sociology moves between examining micro levels of individual issues and macro levels of social problems. The trick is to connect these two levels using what C. Wright Mills called the **sociological imagination** (1959). DIY is a response to contemporary difficulties, and DIYers are using their sociological imaginations to find a solution to alienation, mystification, and loss of community. They are taking back control of their daily lives in startling, creative, and sometimes monumental ways.

DISCUSSION QUESTIONS

1. Do you know someone who is (or are you) a DIY individualist, coordinator, or lifestyler? How is this person different from your other friends?
2. Do you think a little DIY is cool, but a lot of DIY is odd? Where is that line for you, and why do you think it lies where it does?
3. Think of an example of how the lifeworld has been colonized by money or power. How would you go about decolonizing it?

II: Home and Food

The economy is in crisis. Banks are foreclosing on people's homes. The unemployment rate soars to unprecedented levels. Even those who still have work are forced to make drastic concessions to managers seeking reductions. A President offers Hope and Change, but fails to deliver immediate relief. A burgeoning group of disaffected folks who have lost jobs, homes, and faith seek consolation in religion, controlled substances, and demagogues. The year was 1932, and the Great Depression forced many from their homes and farms to become migrant farm workers. At the same time, jobless urbanites looked to rural farming as a solution to their economic woes. In 2009 a similar process occurred with home foreclosures, daunting unemployment levels, and a burgeoning DIY movement in response. Back-to-the-landers are perhaps the quintessential example of a DIY lifestyle group. Waves of DIY back-to-the-land movements have occurred several times in the 20th-century United States, and patterns of continuity and change are revealing about the DIY movement and its social context.

Back to the Land

What Americans might think of as a quintessentially U.S. phenomenon has English antecedents going back over 100 years. Rapid industrialization in England drew farmers and peasants to the factories in cities where conditions were squalid. In his famous essay on the conditions of the working class in 1845 Manchester, Friedrich Engels described streets filled with mud and manure (both human and animal). People lived in makeshift buildings and suffered illness on top of filth. Meanwhile, the emptying of the countryside left it open to decline and misuse. The last of the trees were cut down, agriculture moved towards mono-cropping, and entire villages faded into memory (Gould 1988; Marsh 1982).

For the new city-dwellers, this gave rise to a near-immediate nostalgia for rural life: the city was seen as corrupting to body and soul, while the antidote was found in the countryside and farming. The redemptive lure of rural areas gave rise to the first movement of people away from the city (Gould 1988: ix):

> Back to the Land denotes a dissatisfaction with urban-industrial society and sympathy for things rural and natural, ... self-sufficient and self-governing. ... Back

to Nature conveys notions of the simple life, an alternative to life in the city and work in industry, living in harmony with and as a part of Nature.

The idea of getting back to nature has a long history. Henry David Thoreau found "in nature the redemption of civilization" and walked into the woods to build a home and grow food on the shore of Walden Pond in 1845, making Thoreau perhaps the first American back-to-the-lander. Out West in Yosemite, John Muir declared that the great valleys were more true cathedrals than churches built of brick and mortar.

But as Anglos moved across North America they encountered forests systematically altered by indigenous peoples, who were forcibly moved from their ancestral homes to accommodate western expansion, agriculture, and gold mining. The places we think of as "wild" used to have people living there.

Westward expansion is the major narrative of American history. This frontier story reverberates across the ages, re-enacted again and again. Frederick Jackson Turner, in 1893, wrote his famous essay describing the frontier hypothesis: that the westward movement of people represented a fount of democracy as well as a social safety valve for misfits. The Homestead Act of 1862 offered first-time property acquisition for millions of Americans. This is the opening episode in the back-to-the-land narrative: just on the land, not back to it.

The Homestead Act represented one of the first incarnations of the American Dream. It offered hope to pioneers and gave rise to the idea of the West as a promised land. That notion was still alive even at the height of the Great Depression in 1932 when 40 percent of Americans were still sure that the United States was a "land of opportunity" (Worster 1979: 47). Lured in part by the American Dream, those without work fled to the suburbs and rural areas where, boosters assured them, they could raise animals, grow vegetables, and be self-sufficient and free from the collapsing economic system. The early 20th century back-to-the-land movement had some of the same "push" factors as earlier English antecedents—the corruption and filth of the city—and some of the same "pull" factors—the myth of living close to nature and the American Dream. There were also political pushes, such as attempts to settle cutover lands of the Pacific Northwest and President Roosevelt's Resettlement Administration, which largely led to social and environmental difficulties (Conkin 1967; White 1980). The 1920s saw millions moving from the country to the city in search of jobs, amenities, and freedom from Jim Crow laws. But the period of 1929–1932 was a reversal, with rural areas re-absorbing 1.5 million migrants. Yet, in 1935, there were 2 million rural families on relief (Webb 1983: 335; Woofter 1936). So just as some were leaving the farm due to foreclosure and bankruptcy, following the Okies and exodusters west to the fields of California immortalized in John Steinbeck's *Grapes of Wrath*, others were moving back to the land to escape the ravages of the economic collapse. On the farm they were able to eke out a meager subsistence on rented land. They were doing it themselves out of necessity.

As firms and farms went bankrupt, as unemployment and evictions soared, people helped one another. In some cases they un-evicted themselves—moving back illegally to squat their former property, now owned by the bank. Unemployed Pennsylvania coal miners reopened mines and distributed the coal in the cities for a minimal price, and local juries refused to convict the men of theft of company property (Zinn 1999). In tough times, it seems, people throw off reliance on experts and deference to authority and take matters into their own hands. They come to believe, in the words of Woody Guthrie, that this land is their land.

Woody Guthrie was one of the most visible boosters of the American Dream among the migrant farmers and other back-to-the-landers. Himself an Oklahoma native who followed the farmers, workers, and drifters west during the Great Depression, Guthrie was an inveterate protestor, a socialist, a union supporter, and an itinerant activist (Klein 1980). Guthrie's classic song "This Land is your Land," first written in 1940, described a patriotic vision of America, with "wheat fields waving," "diamond deserts," and "golden valleys." These patriotic symbols, however, are contrasted with the "dust clouds rolling."

The traditional song that most Americans know so well started on a much darker note. The song is a parody of Irving Berlin's "God Bless America," which Guthrie

Figure 2.1 The Woody Guthrie commemorative stamp.
Source: Shutterstock

rewrote as "God Blessed America" (Klein 1980: 140). In addition to the lyrics that schoolchildren know so well, in the original, Guthrie penned the following lines:

> Was a big high wall there that tried to stop me
> A sign was painted said: Private Property.
> But on the back side, it didn't say nothing
> God Blessed America for me.
>
> One bright shiny morning in the shadow of the steeple
> By the relief office I saw my people
> As they stood there hungry,
> I stood there wondering if
> God Blessed America for me.

This version of the song juxtaposes the church and relief office, showing the inability of either to solve the hunger of the American people. In Guthrie's eyes neither officials in Washington or in local government, nor those in the churches were competent. The specter of private property is intimated as the source of the problem: high walls that keep people away from private property lead directly to hungry folks standing in line. Guthrie represents the observer who can cross the walls and see the other side of the signs. Transgressing private property and disobeying warnings would seem to be part of an answer to the nation's problems. It is almost as if Guthrie is urging the listener to violate the law, take back the land, and decolonize the lifeworld.

But the next wave of the back-to-the-land movement in the late 1960s was less economically and more ideologically motivated. Listening to Bob Dylan rather than Woody Guthrie, 1960s activists moved back to the land in part because it was hip, in part because the urban scene was disintegrating, and in part due to economics: a combination of the forces of the 1860s, the 1930s, and new ideals. The first do-it-yourself manuals stem from this era: *Foxfire* and *The Whole Earth Catalog* (published in 1966 and 1968, respectively) taught people how to live simply by making soap, weaving baskets, and to be generally self-reliant as Emerson called for.

Unlike the earlier back-to-the-land movements, that of the late 1960s was largely an ideological counterculture response to growing alienation and disaffection with the establishment. Generally labeled as "hippies," a small wave of activists caught the imagination of journalists and the American people in the period 1968–1970. While salacious news stories about drugs, free love, and communist principles piqued the interest of many readers, the actual number of active back-to-the-landers was never very high. But driven by disillusionment with the more urban examples of 1960s radicalism and the increasingly suburban character of American life, many young people moved back to the land to form do-it-yourself communities centered on farming, voluntary simplicity, and alternative lifestyles. Counter-intuitive as it may seem, the pull of getting back to nature was on the same continuum as urbanites contemporaneously moving to the suburbs. Both were motivated by nostalgic and idealized notions of family farming and Jeffersonian Democracy.

One prime example of a 1960s back-to-the-land movement is "Morningstar," a **commune** 70 miles north of San Francisco near the small town of Sebastopol. Lew Gottlieb founded the commune in the mid-1960s as a place where people could go to "do their own thing." The commune was advertised in San Francisco; hippies, bohemians, and dropouts of all kinds moved north. From the beginning the commune was marked with just what you might expect: growing their own food, building their own houses, and lots of drug use and "free love." In these senses Morningstar was reproduced in many instances across northern California, from Santa Cruz to Humboldt County. But the do-it-yourself mentality did not necessarily gel well with the do-your-own-thing philosophy. Morningstar and many other communes descended into the chaos of heavy drug and alcohol use and physical and sexual violence. Most communes lasted only a few years, dissolving as members moved on (Yablonsky 1968).

Bennett Berger's ethnography of "the Ranch" tells the rare story of the survival of a countercultural community in rural northern California. Driven away from the increased violence and chaos of the Haight-Ashbury scene in San Francisco, several like-minded (and relatively affluent) hippies bought land on the remote northern coast, built a common house, planted a garden, and set about the work of an alternative lifestyle. Berger notes that though there were "push" factors in response to the failed principles from 1967's Summer of Love, there were also "pull" factors of proximity to nature, remoteness, do-it-yourself philosophies, and voluntary simplicity. But when asked if there was "one basic value" that the group adhered to, one hippie replied: "Yes, wash your own dish" (Berger 1981: 30). Being responsible for yourself (washing your own dish) is a radical notion within a social system that encourages hierarchical thinking and the behavioral inequality of hiring people to clean up after us. This, too, is a way of decolonizing our lifeworld by removing money and power from social relationships.

Thus the hippies of the Ranch embodied many of the same impulses to get back to the land and away from a host of real or imagined faults of modern society that framed counterculture attitudes. But unlike most of the communes established in the late 1960s that dissolved as middle-class youths learned the rigors and deficiencies of rural living, the Ranch was able to survive for more than 12 years, weathering many philosophical and ideological storms (Agnew 2004; Berger 1981). This was accomplished, in part, by both flexibility, remoteness, and also what Berger calls "ideological work." A similar commune in Tennessee, the Farm, continues to this day. Perhaps the ultimate in do it yourself is to create your own successful, long-term alternative community.

The lessons that the Ranch and the Farm teach us is that it is possible to live outside the mainstream—to successfully navigate political pressures and individual conflicts in an intensive DIY situation. The hippies of the Ranch exemplify the ability of DIY to be more than just a way of solving the problems of everyday life without the help of experts—we can instead become our own experts. The 1960s back-to-the-land movement shows a more revolutionary political engagement via DIY action, a version of the phrase popular at the time: "The personal is political."

Many people still feel similarly today, and back to the land is very much alive in the 21st century, though with fewer drugs and less free love, and more urban and economic sensibilities. The feeling that "the personal is political" has not diminished. While communes like the Farm still continue, there are broader back-to-the-land and DIY elements seen in community gardens, urban and farming squats, and in Community Supported Agriculture (CSA), where members can spend time working at the farm. These processes all help decolonize the mystery of where food comes from and how to relate directly to producers. And of course there is the reality television show *The Simple Life*. Aired from 2003–2007, the comedy show challenged Paris Hilton and Nicole Richie to work jobs far from their social location, including going back to the land to work on a farm in Arkansas. Though played for laugh lines, *The Simple Life* showed contemporary rural DIY living.

Perhaps the most famous recent example of people moving back to the land is related in Barbara Kingsolver's *Animal, Vegetable, Miracle* (2007). Kingsolver, along with her family, moved to a southern Appalachian farm to consume only that which they could grow themselves or buy locally—a DIY lifestyle that is accessible to some middle-class families. Kingsolver argues that the separation of people from the land was an understandable consequence of industrialization and urbanization: "When we as a nation walked away from the land, our knowledge of food production fell away from us like dirt in a laundry-soap commercial" (2007: 12), which Kingsolver finds regrettable. Though today nearly one-quarter of U.S. households produce some of their own food in a backyard garden (U.S. Census Bureau 2010), by far most of our food calories come from industrial production. This means that food grows on massive, mono-cropped, factory farms and must travel great distances by truck, train, and plane to get to our grocery stores (1,500 miles on average). Some estimate that for every calorie of food nutrition delivered to our plates there are ten calories of petroleum product consumed to get it there (Manning 2004). To address this, Kingsolver gave up processed and transported foods (except each family member chose one exception to maintain sanity—who could live without coffee?). The book is an excellent meditation on the difficulties of such an endeavor, but also on the education and discovery that happen along the way—what Kingsolver calls "miracles."

Attitudes and changes in behavior such as Barbara Kingsolver and her family experienced are widespread and becoming more common. But such miracles of discovery about food are harder to come by in an urban environment. There are, however, back-to-the-land forces in the city as well. People grow, preserve, and enjoy food from backyard and community gardens in thousands of cities across the United States.

Some community gardens are developed specifically for these purposes, while others are "squatted," created by community members from empty lots or other open space. Such gardens not only provide green space in the concrete jungle and nourishing vegetables for local families, they also provide an educational experience for those who participate. The famous chef Alice Waters started a community garden at an elementary school near her Berkeley restaurant Chez Panisse, helping to integrate education about gardening, food, and the environment into the curriculum (the students cook and eat the food for lunch). This is a decolonization of education in a less radical manner than home schooling, but significant in the ways it teaches students about where their food comes from and how to control their diets.

The example of Detroit's inner city is not quite as elegant as a four-star chef starting a community garden at an elementary school, but it's inspiring nonetheless. Detroit's economy in the first decade of the 21st century was in shambles. With several major auto companies bankrupt and assembly plants moving out of town, Detroit's unemployment rate approached 50 percent according to the Mayor. At its high point in 1950, Detroit had almost two million inhabitants, but the current estimate is about 910,000, almost 82 percent African American (U.S. Census Bureau 2009). Foreclosures and abandoned houses blight neighborhoods—in some cases whole blocks are vacant. Those who remain have a median household income of just $29,526 (45

Figure 2.2 A vacant lot becomes a community garden.
Source: Author

percent below the national median) and almost 22 percent of residents are below the poverty line (U.S. Census Bureau 2009). More than half of Detroit's residents live in a "food desert" where access to a grocery store is severely curtailed (Gallagher Group 2007: 4). Amid this social tragedy, "guerilla gardeners" began farming empty lots, creating gardens and feeding fellow residents. Community groups and ad hoc collections of neighbors developed more than 1,000 small farms and community gardens. One farmer even describes it in terms Habermas would understand: "This is a way of decolonizing ourselves from the corporate food structure and doing something better at the same time" (Lee and Abowd 2011). There are similar examples of farming abandoned inner cities in Kansas City, Chicago, Charlotte, and many others.

In Sacramento, the Ron Mandella Community Garden provides a different, more complex example of urban back to the land. The garden started as a normal working-class neighborhood developed in the 1930s with modest California bungalows. In the 1960s as part of a larger plan for the area east of the Capitol, the State condemned one large square block through eminent domain with an eye towards building a complex to house state workers. The existing dwellings were demolished, but by the mid-1970s the plan failed, the area was left vacant and was soon labeled as "urban blight" (Fish 2011; Francis 1987).

What some called blight, however, was an opportunity for community members. They tilled the land into an open garden "guerilla style"—without asking anyone's permission. The City looked the other way for decades and the garden flourished. These DIY coordinators were getting back to the land in a different way from the exodusters of the Depression or the hippies of the 1960s. They still lived and worked in the city, but also committed themselves to growing and enjoying their own food, understanding the rhythms of the seasons and requirements of the soil. They were feeding themselves—without the aid of experts, without permission of the landowner, and for the benefit of the local community.

But in the mid-1990s midtown Sacramento began to bounce back from decades of economic stagnation, and middle-class professionals moved back downtown to be close to shops, cafés, and restaurants. This gentrification process had multiple effects, primarily increasing property values and rents. Poorer residents, including people of color, were forced out. Those who owned their homes or otherwise could afford to stay dealt with a shifting cultural terrain and changing neighborhood values. By the late 1990s the midtown housing market was booming, with real estate prices doubling every few years. The City recognized an opportunity to redevelop the Mandella Gardens into fancy condominiums for middle-class professionals (Fish 2011).

The community gardeners were forced out—first by a fence, then by police patrol. A long battle between the community and the City ensued, and the old phrase "you can't fight City Hall" found meaning yet again. In the end, condominiums were built next to a smaller and highly regulated community garden.

What is interesting about Mandella Gardens is that the State was culpable for creating the "blight" that the City then found it necessary to "fix." The redevelopment agency and City officials could not countenance a community they did not control, one which produced no taxes and served no clearly-defined economic purpose—in fact since people were growing their own food they were not buying it in the stores, a de facto threat to economic growth. The values of the community, those cultural purposes that the garden served, were denied legitimacy. The City had clear values that could be measured in dollars and tallied on spreadsheets, while the community valued more qualitative aspects. Whenever money and power rear their heads, colonization is at work: the community was trying to decolonize their neighborhood and the City saw this as a challenge to its power. Community members were pushed off the land they had attempted to get back to, forced again to shop at the grocery store. The City made the community safe for capitalism again, and the neighborhood lost a vital part of its cultural and social infrastructure. The urban back-to-the-landers were forced to no longer do-it-themselves.

Other urban gardeners are not constrained by property issues. Homeowners who use a portion of their yard to grow a vegetable garden have some of the same motivations as the guerilla gardeners, but they do not have to rely on the beneficence of the

Figure 2.3 Harvesting nature's bounty from the backyard.
Source: Shutterstock

government looking the other way. Though this represents a class-based privilege, it is a widespread one—millions of U.S. households engage in some kind of vegetable gardening, spending $1.4 billion each year to do so (U.S. Census Bureau 2010). This represents a bit of a quandary, as backyard gardeners are clearly buying things in order to do it themselves as DIY individualists or coordinators. They purchase seeds, equipment, and fertilizer. There is a wealth of information online to help the vegetable gardener, but two things are necessary: land and a decent growing season (though container and rooftop gardening is a growing trend, and artificial lights have helped overcome short seasons).

Backyard gardeners share many characteristics with both hippie back-to-the-landers and guerrilla gardeners. They can produce high-quality vegetables for a fraction of the grocery store price, and many find the yard work therapeutic. Preserving the harvest, however, is a different story. Produce from the garden, the farmers' market, or the grocery store all have a similar shelf life—use it or lose it. Today, however, almost all vegetables are shipped great distances year-round. Produce that can be grown in this hemisphere's summer is transported half a world away during the off-season. It might not taste like much, but year-round availability exerts a powerful force on our psyches—we see the fresh red tomato in winter, and we *want* it. While cans of vegetables lining store shelves may be an acceptable alternative for the long winter months, there is another option being re-discovered by the new generation of do-it-yourselfers: canning.

Canning is the preservation of food through control of the bacteria that cause food to spoil. Rot is slowed by refrigeration or nearly stopped by freezing, but these preservation techniques are limited by space and the cost of energy. The far more simple technology of canning comes from before refrigerators were common. Canning kills bacteria or inhibits growth with simple techniques: water-bath canning raises the food temperature nearly to boiling, killing the bacteria. Produce is transferred to glass jars (also sterilized in boiling water), self-sealing caps are applied, and the finished jars are processed in boiling water again. The resulting jar can be stored for years. Do-it-yourself canners side-step garden seasonality and enjoy their harvest through the winter.

In fact, now they can also share this bounty. There are many health code requirements to meet before one can sell food. This involves high costs that most people can't or won't meet, and represents the same barrier to DIY as building codes do for home fixers. The most recent movements in DIY food are illegal markets for home-prepared local food. In San Francisco, The Underground Market meets monthly in clandestine locations to avoid the scrutiny of authorities. Venues are distributed via Twitter, blogs, and an email distribution list. The Underground Market represents a "DIY resistance movement against the bureaucratic, corporate-run, food vendor governance board that says people cannot sell homemade dishes in a public venue without a license" (Pallo 2011). Similar markets using this model are popping up in cities around the nation.

The back-to-the-land movement has had several incarnations over the last century, from exodusters to urban gardeners. Some went back to the land for the principle of being close to nature, others did it for economic or community reasons. What is common to all of these movements is the DIY perspective—in Habermas's terms, these DIY foodies are decolonizing the lifeworld by removing corporations, government, and experts from the most basic of human activities: nourishing our bodies with healthy food.

Fixer-Uppers and House-Flippers

DIY at home comes in many forms other than food provision. Perhaps the most ubiquitous is the fix-it-yourself home project. DIYers have a tremendous resource for step-by-step instructions on the Internet; the website www.doityourself.com is a prime example. Giving tips for projects from landscaping to electrical wiring, it is a wealth of information for the home improvement DIYer, though it offers the disclaimer that all information is provided "as is." Fixer-uppers can also get information from the DIY Network on cable. The network's shows are long on drama but short on details: catering to the current fad of ordinary things remade to be extraordinary, the DIY Network features shows such as *The House Crashers, The Rehab Addict*, and *I Hate My Kitchen*. The network helps to build desires for home improvements while offering little effective help (it would seem difficult to follow tips once you're out in the yard away from the television). The network website, however, has a listing of professional service providers—presumably for when you're in over your head. Also on the website are products highlighted on recent shows, with convenient links to online stores. The DIY Network may want people to fix it themselves, but they are part of the broader capitalist economic system. To this extent they represent Habermas's "system" recolonizing the lifeworld. Cable shows and websites are a resource for DIYers, but also a way to draw them back into consumption: people are rarely able to leave the system and become entirely self-reliant in the manner of Thoreau or Emerson. Instead, the DIY process is continually coopted back into the market.

This is nowhere more evident than the phenomenon of "flipping a house." Entrepreneurial people take advantage of low mortgage rates and a booming housing market to buy a "fixer-upper," renovate it, then resell or "flip" the house within a short period of time at a much-increased sale price. Though contractors have been doing this for some time, the idea exploded in the last decade—to the extent that two reality television shows on the topic became successful.

This is DIY taken to a capitalist extreme. The hosts of the shows were not doing it themselves to enjoy a new living situation, they were in it for the money. As this phenomenon gained popularity, building on the American Dream of something-for-nothing, viewership grew by leaps and bounds. This fad, however, was necessarily

Figure 2.4 A DIY house-flipper.
Source: Shutterstock

short-lived as the housing market crumbled, mortgage loans became scarce, and people's real incomes vanished with the economic crisis of 2008.

Where do **house-flippers** go to buy their materials and seek advice? The two largest building materials retailers in the United States are The Home Depot and Lowe's. Both companies suffered in the global recession of 2008–2009, as DIYers dropped the priority of home improvement projects. In 2009 Home Depot sales were down 7.2 percent and Lowe's sales were down 2.1 percent, but both companies were back in positive territory in 2010. According to annual reports and quarterly earnings statements, net sales for The Home Depot were up 2.8 percent in 2010, and Lowe's were up 3.4 percent. Both companies were profitable and expanded their reach by opening new stores.

Lowe's 2009 Annual Report to shareholders is particularly revealing as to how they understand the DIY market:

Consumers have also shifted to more Do-It-Yourself (DIY) projects; balancing the tradeoffs of convenience versus the cost. Our surveys through secondary research indicate that the home is still very important to consumers and it is still most consumers' largest asset, even with the declines in home values they have suffered over recent years. And more importantly, the psychological attachment to the home and what it stands for remains strong.

(Lowe's Companies, Inc. 2009: 18)

Lowe's contextualizes its lower sales and earnings for shareholders in this language, but also recognizes why people engage in DIY home improvements: the home is generally a family's largest asset and people have a strong emotional connection to the place they live. In tough economic times, many homeowners are discovering their inner DIYer:

This resurgence of do-it-yourself (DIY) has many homeowners tackling projects for the first time, and we have increased staffing levels accordingly to ensure we are ready to serve customers and provide knowledgeable advice.

(Lowe's Companies, Inc. 2009: 1)

What is striking about this passage from Lowe's Annual Report is its explicit recognition that customers are DIYers, and its savvy understanding that staff may need to walk these first-timers through the process.

The Lowe's Annual Report for 2009 reveals that the DIY customer is central to its marketing plan and continued profitability. Lowe's understands the shifts in the economy and how consumers are likely to respond. DIYers and house-flippers are the core base for these companies, and the resurgence of the DIY movement is responsible for their tremendous growth. This clearly shows that DIYers are shifting payment from a contractor to a home improvement superstore.

The Entrepreneurial Twist

Like flipping houses, doing it yourself can sometimes become a full-time job. The **entrepreneurial** twist to DIY comes when people realize that they can make money from doing it themselves. There are many entrepreneurial offshoots of the DIY movement: a weekly bazaar of handmade goods in Eugene Oregon called the Saturday Market, the arts and crafts website Etsy, and DIY conferences like Maker Faire.

Eugene, Oregon is home to a vibrant arts and crafts community, perhaps born from the vestiges of the hippie scene of the 1960s. In conjunction with a large farmers' market, every weekend more than 300 crafters, knitters, silk-screeners, and jewelry-makers converge on downtown Eugene for the Saturday Market. A wide variety of goods are for sale, from original artwork to tie-dyed shirts. Food carts fulfill shoppers'

Figure 2.5 Vegetables for sale at the Eugene Saturday Market.
Source: Shutterstock

cravings, and a small stage features several local musicians. Begun in 1970, the Market is now a non-profit with an annual budget of $450,000 per year. The artisans of the Saturday Market adhere to standards created by a volunteer community, which reflect demystification in that the maker must be the seller and artwork must be original. The Eugene Saturday Market is a place where entrepreneurial local artists can sell their crafts and unite in a community of like-minded lifestyle DIYers.

On a broader scale, the website Etsy is a clearinghouse for handcrafted goods. With everything from hand-knit scarves to hand-sewn organic dog chew toys, the artisans of Etsy sell DIY products. The mission of Etsy (2010) is

> to enable people to make a living making things, and to reconnect makers with buyers. Our vision is to build a new economy and present a better choice: Buy, Sell, and Live Handmade.

Like the Saturday Market, connecting "makers with buyers" means that Etsy helps demystify where commodities come from, and removes the alienation of the mediated social relationship by bringing producers and consumers together. This is a decolonization of the lifeworld, and yet it is not without its own tension: Etsy is a for-profit corporation. The lifestyler artisans of Etsy sell their goods online, and the corporation takes a share of the transaction. Again we see the simultaneous decolonization of the lifeworld and the immediate cooptation by enterprising capitalists. It is a double-edged sword: artists need a marketplace to sell their products, but not everyone has access to a resource like Eugene's Saturday Market. For a price, the entrepreneurs at Etsy provide a solution.

Unlike its online sister, Maker Faire is a face-to-face gathering of crafters. Started near San Francisco in 2006 as an offshoot of *MAKE* magazine (published by O'Reilly Media), every year several Maker Faires are held in cities across the United States. The Faire is designed to "celebrate arts, crafts, engineering, science projects and the Do-It-Yourself (DIY) mindset." Topics include "rockets & robots, diy science & technology, arts & crafts, bicycles, electronics, artisan foods, urban farming, sustainable living, woodworking" and many others (Maker Faire 2010). Similar to Etsy, the Maker Faire is a product of entrepreneurs who want to help DIY lifestylers recognize themselves as a community. Like Etsy, it represents a recolonization of the lifeworld by capitalist forces.

There are many other contemporary examples of DIY home and food—not for sale, but for gifts, personal use, and the simple pleasure of doing it yourself. The modern arts and crafts movement includes quilters, knitters, and other individualist and coordinator crafters. A wide array of businesses cater to such DIY crafters, from JoAnne Fabrics and Michael's craft stores to authors like Amy Sedaris who recently published *Simple Times: Crafts for Poor People* (2010). In the book, Sedaris discusses ways to make crafts and redecorate on a budget that doesn't quite reach that of Martha Stewart. Entrepreneurs within our capitalist economy continually seek a way to exploit niche markets. Whether it is a magazine, a retail supply store, or an online clearinghouse, capitalism continually finds ways to coopt movements that on their face threaten the profit of traditional corporations. In this respect, DIY is not so different from the cooptation of the **punk rock** image by mall retailers like Hot Topic, or the use of the rebel image of bike messengers to sell bicycle bags to commuters (Wehr 2009).

Conclusion

In the most personal realms of how we feed ourselves, remodel our home, and spend our spare time, the do-it-yourself movement shows that people in the United States are very much concerned with issues of self-reliance. Whether motivated by a political perspective or simple economics, people are doing it themselves in a wide array of venues. Though not everyone can move back to the land or create a commune, Americans fix up their own houses, garden, preserve their own food, and enjoy arts and crafts in their spare time. Some of them even make a living at it.

The DIY movement represents a shift away from relying on professionals towards self-reliance and independence from the larger systems of governance and capitalism—Habermas's decolonization of the lifeworld. People are doing it themselves and taking back what they have relinquished to the service sector. But the forces of capitalism are strong, and entrepreneurs have found a way to coopt the DIY movement by offering

DIY-lite goods and services. This brings DIYers back into the market just as many back-to-the-landers returned to the city. In the next chapter we will see how the portions of our lives made up by school and work offer some resistance to these forces of cooptation.

DISCUSSION QUESTIONS

1. Do you think you could move back to the land? What would it take to make that work in your life? Would you be willing to give up non-local food to eat only what you could produce?
2. Can you think of ways that your family or friends engage in DIY behaviors like fixing up the house or crafting? In what ways are these examples of DIY, or DIY-lite?
3. Would you choose a DIY-related job if you could? What would you do yourself if you could make a living from it?

III: School and Work

In the 21st century, Americans and people the world over are working from home, schooling their own children, and engaging in self-organized leisure activities more than ever before. Though many of the same themes are apparent in these realms of life, as in back-to-the-land movements, some things are markedly different. The simple economic truth that DIY is often cheaper still applies, as does the more political response that everyday life is colonized by the faceless power of the market. But there are also reasons of **ideology**, fear of the government, and the desire to protect ourselves from unknown or unseen hazards of modern life.

Along with the many medical and technological advancements of modern life come many threats to the health of our families: environmental pollutants in the air, water, and food; strangers in the city who might take our children; global climate change, and others. We generally respond by retreating to the marketplace. We buy bottled water rather than pressure our municipal utility to provide clean tap water. We buy a more fuel-efficient car, or reduce our carbon footprint by buying emission-offset credits. Andrew Szasz (2007) has called this "shopping our way to safety," a goal we can sadly never fully achieve. These consumption behaviors represent ways in which our reactions are subsumed back into being functional and profitable for capitalism.

But there are other responses. Rather than putting children into the arms of strangers, Americans have increasingly developed neighborhood childcare groups—banding together, getting to know one another, and trusting other parents rather than a service provider within the larger market economy. Faced with the high price of gas and tolls, some commuters choose to reduce their carbon footprint by joining a "casual carpool" where strangers meet at a common location—some in need of a ride and others with extra space in their car. The drivers take advantage of reduced tolls and quicker commutes in a carpool lane, while riders benefit from a faster and cheaper ride.

The casual carpool certainly helps to reduce our carbon footprint but driving a vehicle that does not run on fossil fuels clearly achieves this end more efficiently. Many people now brew their own biodiesel using vegetable oil recycled from fast food deep fryers. With any standard diesel vehicle, drivers can move outside the fossil fuel economy and commute to work with less guilt (though one hopes they pick up folks from the casual carpool as well!).

Psychologists have eased the pressures of life for at least 100 years; yet recently people have addressed these needs through group-based peer counseling or by consulting self-help books. There are many areas of DIY behavior that meet people's needs outside of reliance on experts, professionals, or the larger market economy. This chapter explores several key examples of DIY in the daily experiences of school, work, and play.

Home Schooling

One of the most interesting things about the DIY movement is its astonishing diversity of political perspectives. As we saw in Chapter II, back-to-the-landers might be free-love hippies or middle-class urbanites. DIY schooling is similar: on one end of the spectrum some schools require volunteer time from parents, and on the other end there are parents who take on all aspects of their children's education, schooling them completely at home. The popular media presents a stereotype of these parents as politically conservative, predominantly rural, and highly religious. But this stereotype is not borne out in reality. **Home schooling** is more common in rural areas, but there are progressive, liberal, middle-of-the road, and conservative home-schoolers. Some, perhaps most, are religious, but many outspoken home-schoolers do not belong to any organized religion.

Home schooling was, of course, the norm in the United States until the early 1900s when public education became widespread. The laudable goals of public education have always been roughly threefold: to produce well-educated people, to encourage an informed citizenry, and to inspire individual ambition. This idea fits well with the stories we are told about democracy and meritocracy—that a good democracy requires an educated populace, and the most meritorious will succeed and be rewarded. No less than Alexis de Tocqueville and James Dewey argued in favor of such ideas. But there was dissent even at the dawn of public education. H. L. Mencken (1924) wrote that the true aim of public education is not to encourage knowledge and intelligence in children, but to

> reduce as many individuals as possible to the same safe level, to breed and train a standardized citizenry, to put down dissent and originality.

Suspicion of public schools has always been with us, but the social crises of the middle 20th century brought class-based and racial fears to the forefront. Some argued that schools were meant only to prepare students for menial work in blue-collar jobs. Others argued that the Supreme Court's reversal of racial segregation would adversely affect the quality of education. Fears and suspicions repeatedly surfaced over the last 50 years, with only slight changes in nuance or target. The current movement towards charter schools, privatization, and home schools are but another response to recurrent fears, legitimate or not (Blacker 1998; Bowles and Gintis 1976; Gatto 2003).

In the 1970s approximately 20,000 students were home schooled, a number which grew to perhaps 200,000 by the 1980s. By 2001 home-schooled students numbered about 1.7 million, and in the last ten years this has likely doubled (Aurini and Davies 2005: 462; Romanowski 2001). Brian Ray (1997: 41) reports that these students are predominantly White (96 percent), but also 1.5 percent Hispanic, 1 percent Asian/ Pacific Islander, 0.5 percent American Indian, and 0.5 percent African American. As one might expect, in school districts where there is higher public expenditure on education there is less home schooling. But a strong effect is also seen in the average educational attainment of parents—districts with higher parental education have higher rates of home schooling (Houston and Toma 2003: 931–32).

People choose to school their children at home for a wide variety of reasons. Romanowski (2001: 79) describes two categories: "ideologues," who object to what is being taught in public schools, and "pedagogues," who believe that they can teach their children better than public school teachers. The ideologues do so for religious reasons or a suspicion of humanism in public schools (though Houston and Toma found that religious adherence did not show a statistical effect on home schooling rates). The pedagogues suspect that their children will not receive the attention they deserve—due to the special needs of the student or the constraints of the school. But in addition to these two categories, there are parents who home school their children out of fear. This fear could be of the teachers who are bored or burned out, or of potential pedophiles. Some people home school their children out of a fear of what public education can or can't offer. There are also anti-institutionalists who feel constrained by a generic education for their children.

As part of this project, I interviewed home-schooling parents and adults who were home schooled as children to gain more insight into this diversity. It quickly became apparent that most of them are committed and careful parents, though there were a few outliers (the hippie parents who didn't much like school and taught their kids how to grow marijuana). But far and away the majority of parents had principled and righteous reasons for home schooling their children. All but one of the responding parents were female, which shows the gendered imbalance of home schooling: just as with primary schooling generally, it is women who home school their children. Though both parents in dual-parent households normally make the decision, home schooling becomes another component of women's domestic labor.

One mother who home schooled her six children had a careful and thoughtful approach after majoring in education as an undergraduate student:

> I saw that in some classes, due to class size or the individual needs of a select few students, there would be some students who would be completely overlooked and the teacher would be unable to discern those students' individual personalities and/or needs.

Figure 3.1 Do-it-yourself schooling.
Source: Shutterstock

Another mother had strong feelings about local public schools:

> The public schools where I lived … were horrid. I lost my job and could not afford to pay the private school tuition that I had been paying.

Yet another said:

> Public schools just have too much politics and bureaucracy attacking them from all sides to be able to properly educate our kids.

These mothers show the range of responses—all are supremely concerned with the quality of education that their children would get in a public school, from the micro level of interaction to the macro level of politics.

One common reason for home schooling is the feeling that public education cannot meet the needs of all children, especially for students at the statistical margins on either side—gifted or bored. One mother told me a heart-wrenching story of her child who was thought by their teacher to have ADHD and to need medication. A doctor diagnosed the child as bright, but bored:

> We soon realized that with public schools these days there is a box, a very small box. If a child does not fit into this box then they do not thrive. Schools just aren't equipped with enough resources or money to deal with children outside of the box.

This mother went through a process that too many are familiar with. She attempted to work with the schools as best she could, but to no avail. For this family at least, home schooling was a better decision than medication.

Before undertaking home schooling the parents researched the topic and prepared extensively. They "read books written by others who had taught their children at home" and "contrasted and compared a variety of home school curricula."

Home-schoolers have many resources at their disposal, including the online clearinghouse for home-schooling materials and information, www.homeschool.com, where the home-schooling parent can find lesson plans, workbooks, and motivational support. The site encourages many of the same principles as private, non-mainstream educational organizations like Montessori and Waldorf, such as individual learning styles and progress. What is different, of course, is that it is up to the parent to recognize these aspects of their children rather than trained professional teachers.

Children of home-schooled parents are generally positive about their experiences, highlighting the benefits of having a mom/teacher: "home school was a great experience for me because my teacher was so accessible." But this begs the question of how these families navigate the dual roles of teacher/mother and child/student.

The transition back to public school (which most home-schooled children do around ninth grade) can be fraught with difficulty. Critics of home schooling argue that children will be improperly socialized, or that the biases of the parents will not receive a counterbalance from teachers and peers. But most of the home-schooled adults that I spoke with did not see it this way at all:

> Most of my friends went to church with me anyway, so I didn't feel left out socially. I made the transition to private school in the ninth grade and then transferred to public schools later in high school. Looking back, I had been a bit sheltered from bullying, peer pressure, and more negative influences that public school provides. Now, as a public school teacher, I understand why my parents did not want to subject my siblings or me to a public school environment or curriculum. There are multiple flaws to our public educational system and the curriculum that is being taught in schools (such as teachers not following frameworks, holes in curriculum—vertically and horizontally, lack of discipline and low expectations of students, unqualified teachers, etc.) that I have serious qualms about ever sending any children I would have in the future to a public school.

This remarkable woman was home schooled and then became a public school teacher—and one who "has serious qualms" with putting her own children through public school. She has a clear and strong critique of public education, perhaps as taught by her mother but also from her own experience.

Other students had a more difficult time with the transition:

The transition for me was on the more difficult side at first. … Mostly, interacting with other students, dealing with multiple subjects for a much lengthier time period, learning to read a variety of teachers for moods and expectations was all new to me.

This former home-school student has a perceptive take on what it means to be a successful public education student. In the public system students need to be as attentive to their teachers as they do to the material being presented.

Home-schooling parents take their children's education into their own hands and devote a significant portion of their lives and livelihoods to the cause. The parents I spoke with found it a worthwhile investment, and most of the children viewed it as a positive experience in hindsight. By definition, these folks are consummate DIYers. Like home gardeners or house-flippers, they are doing it themselves without oversight by experts. Unlike the home gardener, if they make a mistake they can't just compost the plants and try again next year.

Interestingly, many home-schoolers and the home schooled do not consider themselves the DIY type. One adult who was home schooled related an emblematic tale:

I do not identify myself as a DIY type. However, I do believe that "necessity is the mother of invention." These reasons don't make us classic DIY-ers, as I understand them. We're just doing what we have to do, given whatever factors are presented to us. We're the Do-It-Yourself-If-You-Have-To type!

Perhaps this is an apt label—home-schoolers do not necessarily fall into the broader DIY lifestyle, but when it comes to the education of their children they feel as if they have no choice. The stakes are just too high and they become the "Do-It-Yourself-If-You-Have-To type." However, perhaps we can all learn from the response of two home-schooled children aged seven and nine. As part of the survey their father asked if they considered themselves DIY type of people (I intended these questions for adults who had been home schooled, but was misunderstood in this case). Their father told me that they said yes and thought the question was funny—"Who wouldn't be?"

So how do home-schoolers fit into the DIY typology? As discussed in Chapter 1, when it comes to DIY there are individualists, coordinators, and lifestylers. Some engage in DIY behavior for relatively simple and personal reasons such as reducing financial expenditures or appreciating the flavor of homegrown food. Others have a broader critique of institutions and the social system, which they want to resist in coordination with others. Some take the idea as far as it will go and embrace a DIY lifestyle. Home-schoolers fall into all three categories. Some parents choose to teach their children themselves because of personal reasons regarding faith and spirituality. Others see themselves as "not an institution person" and want to offer their children a more specialized education tailored to their specific needs.

This latter group is clearly acting to decolonize their educational world. Just as the Black Panthers set up community schools in the 1960s, these parents feel that the government cannot offer what their children need. Though they do not put it in these exact terms, they see some truth to the radical critique that public education simply trains a new generation to enter the workforce as cogs in the machine. These cogs have no need for creativity, genius, or personality. They need only know how to sit quietly for eight hours at a stretch, not ask too many questions, and stay in line. Public schools thus meet the needs of capitalism and representational governance—they produce normalized citizens capable of working and voting, but not capable of developing a sustained radical critique of the system.

John Taylor Gatto (2003) is an outspoken critic of public education and the ways in which it stifles creative thought. He was a career public high school teacher, and in reflection he concluded:

> After a long life, and thirty years in the public school trenches, I've concluded that genius is as common as dirt. We suppress our genius only because we haven't yet figured out how to manage a population of educated men and women. The solution, I think, is simple and glorious. Let them manage themselves.

Perhaps we need to manage ourselves a little more, and submit to management a little less.

Thinking Outside the Cubicle

One way to manage ourselves more is to fire our boss and work for ourselves, either solo or as part of a collective. Enabled by the expansion of relatively inexpensive and fast Internet connections, people are working from home more than ever before. What was a relatively rare situation just ten years ago, working from home for a day or two of the workweek has become common in some white-collar professions (I am working from home as I write this). Some people work almost completely offsite, even living in another state and commuting to work one day a month by airplane.

To meet the unusual needs of this professional class, an array of DIY services has developed, including self-publishing firms, co-working spaces, and websites that offer online meeting space and communication services. The concept of co-working is a communal space where independent professionals can work on their own projects. Claiming to "redefine the way we do work," a supportive website describes the idea that: "independent professionals and those with workplace flexibility work better together than they do alone" (Co-working Wiki 2011).

The Urban Hive in Sacramento is a location for such professionals to work where they are not subject to the distractions of home. Exhorting the work-at-home professional to "think outside the cubicle" and "connect, share, collaborate, create," the

Figure 3.2 The Urban Hive, Sacramento.
Source: Author

Urban Hive offers an infrastructure for independent professionals to socialize with others in a non-office environment: "think of it as a great company culture, just without the company" (2011). The Urban Hive opened in 2009, when there were just 12 similar spaces nationwide. Of those 12 only six remain, but 100 more have sprung up. Responding to the isolation of the work-at-home professional, the Urban Hive offers space, community, and coffee—like many offices but with "cool coworkers" instead of cubicles.

Another DIY job that is outside the cubicle is the delivery service offered by the bicycle messenger. Cupid Courier Collective in San Francisco is a special kind of bicycle messenger company—a **worker cooperative**. They operate with "true equality of effort and profit," where every courier "can handle all aspects of the business" from phone dispatching to accounting. They offer the standard services of most bicycle messenger companies, but make an appeal to liberal San Franciscans to choose the "savvy democratic workplace" of a worker cooperative. This messenger cooperative has taken a DIY job and made it even more DIY by handling the business themselves. Without a separation between workers and managers, the couriers at Cupid step outside the capitalist system and its byproduct, worker alienation. Though they clearly still work within capitalism by taking money for services rendered, they offer a different vision of how work can be organized in the modern moment.

The San Francisco Bay Area is home to many other worker cooperatives, from coffee shops to pizza restaurants to—believe it or not—a high school and a strip club.

Worker cooperatives (sometimes also called worker collectives) generally conform to a democratic and egalitarian organization. Instead of having owners, managers, and workers arrayed in a hierarchical structure, worker cooperatives have a flat organization. All workers gain from the business through profit sharing, and decisions are made by the collective rather than a top-down process. Worker collectives challenge the traditional mode of doing business in a capitalist economy by allowing workers themselves to benefit from their labor—the harder they work, the more profits they share. This incentive structure undoes the alienation of a traditional capitalist industry, and demystifies the decision process and the profit structure. Workers understand the centrality of their involvement and act accordingly. If everyone pulls together, they all win. This is a political decision to sidestep the competitive structure of capitalism, and is a further decolonization of the world of work.

Worker collectives in the United States go back to at least the 1840s, though they were rare until the 20th century (Jones 1984: 38). They are owned and managed by workers, with equal pay (regardless of type of work), rotating job assignments, and distribution of profits in the form of wages (Craig and Pencavel 1992: 1083–6). Cooperatives are found in diverse sectors, from dairy coops in the Midwest, to coffee growers in Central America (Curl 2009; Ellerman 1984). In the Pacific Northwest there are lumber and plywood cooperatives that date back to the 1920s and represent one of the longest enduring worker-owned sectors of the U.S. manufacturing economy (Greenberg 1984).

William Foote Whyte helped found the sociological study of worker collectives by examining Mondragón, a system of worker production cooperatives started by five men in 1956 in the now autonomous Basque region of Spain. Twenty years later it had expanded to 65 firms with nearly 15,000 worker-members (Johnson and Whyte 1977). Ten years after that, despite an economic recession, there were 87 firms with more than 18,000 members (Whyte 1982: 2). Mondragón is based on a foundation of two key industrial collectives: a foundry and a metal working company. The area has a long history of industrial capacity dating back to the famed swords of Toledo, the steel for which was smelted in the Mondragón area (Whyte and Whyte 1988: 25). Founded in a democratic manner through the dedicated work of Don José María, the first classes for workers were in the early 1940s and the first worker cooperatives in the middle 1950s took on the well-established anti-union industries in town and slowly overwhelmed them. The steady growth of cooperatively run firms in the area spiraled upwards on this foundation of social cohesion.

Mondragón solves several problems that typically plague worker collectives, including how to expand and persist in the broader market, how to distribute the wealth created by the cooperatives, and how to maintain equality amongst workers. The workers of Mondragón creatively achieved an enviable profitability and growth record through employment creation and worker education, and by re-investing funds in the cooperative that would have been appropriated as profit by owners. Profitability is higher than in normal private corporations, and worker absenteeism much lower. Fiscal surpluses (profit) are distributed between the collective's reserves and individual workers. Furthermore, there is a maximum pay differential between the lowest and highest paid worker, famously set at three-to-one, along with set-asides for social security. Mondragón has met the two major criteria for success of a worker cooperative: it has persisted and it has remained democratic with the principle of one worker, one vote (Morrison 1991: 173; Thomas and Logan 1982: 50, 118–43; Whyte and Whyte 1988). If there is any one thing that enabled the success of Mondragón and other worker cooperatives, it is this principle of democracy and collectivism. Workers can succeed when they band together to do it themselves.

Worker-owned cooperatives or collectives rise and fall with the economy. Sometimes they rise, weather some storms, then fail when a recession hits. The Berkeley cooperative supermarket is an example of this. Established in 1929 from a group of several buyer's clubs, "The Co-op," as it was usually called, bloomed, expanded, and then finally failed in the recession of the 1980s (Curl 2009). Other cooperatives were born specifically out of recessions: the Weirton Steel Mill in West Virginia was put up for sale by the parent company, National Steel, and eventually offered to the workers: "What they're telling us is to either buy it or lose it." The workers bought the company, which was the fundamental economic engine of the entire town, saying "If this mill goes, so does the town" (Varano 1999: 3, 87). What is odd about many large employee-owned corporations, like United Airlines, is that they still have management, unions, and labor strife. Though the workers technically own them, this does not necessarily translate into worker democracy. It is not quite DIY.

The more contemporary example of Argentina's worker-run factories caught the imagination of many progressives in the middle-2000s when Avi Lewis and Naomi Klein released the film *The Take*. Along with many nations around the world, Argentina's economy hit bottom in 2001. The crisis was especially deep due to years of political corruption and mismanagement of the banking and financial sectors (lavaca collective 2007). Over a period of months, there was a run on the banks, inflation skyrocketed, and major corporations crashed. The effects rippled through the economy, with working people affected more harshly than others as factories were shuttered and work disappeared. But like the Pennsylvania coal miners in America's Great Depression, workers in Argentina did something different: they went back to work at the closed factories. Negotiating for title to the physical plant in exchange for back wages, first one, then another, finally over 150 factories were re-made into worker cooperatives. This allowed production to continue as the workers sold their goods for lower costs—just enough to cover wages and materials. In some cases they even donated materials to help rebuild schools and community centers. The workers were doing it by themselves and for themselves, not governed by the bosses or producing for the owners. They were also doing it for the community (lavaca collective 2007).

But worker collectives do not have to be part of a grand heroic movement. In Berkeley a private high school is run by the teachers themselves. Maybeck High School claims to offer "a unique opportunity for students to engage with an academically challenging college-preparatory curriculum in a collaborative rather than competitive environment." They are able to provide this, they argue, because of the nature of their organization:

> As a teacher-run school, Maybeck places great emphasis on the autonomy of its teachers within the classroom. We believe that when teachers are encouraged to shape their lessons freely, they invest themselves fully in their teaching and engage their students most effectively.

Though it is unclear whether success derives from workplace organization or the class bias inherent with the $24,000/year tuition, Maybeck students have been successful gaining acceptance to competitive universities (http://www.maybeckhs.org/).

Perhaps the most revealing worker collective in the San Francisco Bay Area is the Lusty Lady strip club in the North Beach neighborhood. This part of town is close to the old harbor, and it has seen the type of licentious community that grew organically near the docks of major seaports, from jazz halls and gin joints to whorehouses and, so they say, pirate dens. The Lusty Lady started in 1976, and was somewhat counter-intuitively known to hire independent and intelligent women. In 1997, after a difficult struggle, the "live nude girls" united to form a union, allying with the Service Employees International Union (*Live Nude Girls Unite!* 2000). But in 2003 the owners decided to close the business. The union workers purchased the club and found out, up close and personal, the difficulties of running a strip club in an equitable and democratic manner.

The workers of the Lusty Lady nicely summarize the challenges of running a worker cooperative (Lusty Lady 2011):

> Although worker ownership is a rare and ideal situation, it is not without its challenges. … How will we make the decision to move forward and be certain the wishes and intentions of the majority of members are represented?

The work of a collective is difficult. There is normal administrative work required to run a business, but also the important task of making major decisions. There are organizational questions to be considered: how are votes to be structured? Will a small sub-group be tasked with daily operations, and if so will they become boss-like? True democracy takes a long time. The dancers of the Lusty Lady point out the problems of democracy, but also the benefits of doing it yourself (Lusty Lady 2011):

> There are decisions to make and votes to count and seemingly endless meetings and discussions to be had. And if we want something done (employee manuals,

new carpet, a soda machine) we have to do it ourselves. But the beauty of it is, we do. Somehow, the decision gets made and the new idea gets implemented and we get the new carpet.

Decolonizing the lifeworld isn't easy. Worker collectives take a lot of effort to be successful. The strippers of the Lusty Lady demonstrate the high level of commitment it takes to run a worker-owned business while not reproducing the same authority structures of capitalism.

What the cooperatives of the San Francisco Bay Area show is that workers are limited only by their own imagination. If high school teachers, pizza bakers, bike messengers, and strippers can successfully do it themselves, we all can—even a bunch of punk kids.

Self-Organized Play

Down near the bayfront in Berkeley is a music club known simply by its address: 924 Gilman Street is an all-ages venue run collectively without any goal of profit. It has been a site of choice for punk bands for more than 25 years, and it is still running strong (Edge 2004). 924 Gilman demonstrates that cooperatives can span any sector of society, and the do-it-yourself attitude extends to leisure time as well as school or work.

From the beginning, Gilman has been a collective where members are charged $2 per year and are expected to come to meetings and make informed decisions. Gilman has also always been a "straight edge" venue, averse to drugs, alcohol, and violence. Politically progressive, the collective decreed that there would be no racism, homophobia, sexism, or corporate music—Gilman would be fully independent. Gilman was the launching pad for many bands that would become internationally known, including Neurosis, Operation Ivy, Rancid, and Green Day. In keeping with their fiercely independent streak, bands that have signed to major record labels are not welcome to perform or attend—even bands like Green Day that might like to play a nostalgic show (Edge 2004).

Leisure time might seem like an odd form of DIY behavior. After all, isn't all leisure time DIY? Certainly much of it is, from the local softball league to the pickup basketball game. But an increasing amount of leisure time is not DIY. Think of the classic date: dinner at a restaurant, a movie afterwards, or the bar later—in all of these activities we rely on others to do the work for us. When out on a date this might make sense, after all the point is to relax and enjoy each other's company. But we can also see how capitalism has colonized our leisure time in this example and many others: the ball game, the organized bus tour, the visit to a casino, wine-tasting … so many of our leisure activities are structured by others who extract a fee from us for our entertainment. The staggering dollar salaries of most professional athletes and the Hollywood celebrity spectacles should give us pause—where is that money coming from? It comes from all of us of course. We pay to see them play, we watch commercials, and then (the marketers hope) buy products. Our leisure time is not immune from colonization—some people's idea of a good relaxing weekend day is spent at the mall.

How do we entertain ourselves? In places like 924 Gilman, in local self-organized sports, and even online we can see people moving outside of this model of relying on others to entertain us. People self-organize entertainment in a variety of forms, from the traditional quilting bee or back-porch party to geo-caching and the online meet-up.

Perhaps the best example of re-envisioning entertainment is the concept of vacation. The self-help publishing world has churned out vacation guidebooks for some time. Fifty years ago *Let's Go* and *Dollar a Day* blazed the trail for contemporary guides like *Lonely Planet*. These books tell the would-be solo traveler how to avoid standard bus tours. They tell the reader "must-see" locations, but also describe how to get off the beaten path—creating a whole new beaten path of "Lonely Planeteer" tourists, each toting their dog-eared guides.

The Internet also offers an instant community for those seeking esoteric activities. The sites Meet Up and Craigslist provide a free platform for people to broadcast their ideas for DIY play activities, and the category has proliferated remarkably in recent times. Craigslist provides readers a forum on pretty much anything, from requests for

Figure 3.3 A "Lonely Planeteer" traveling DIY-style.
Source: Shutterstock

athletes ("Female softball player needed TONIGHT") to requests for crafting part-
ners ("Love to bead? Want to bead together?"). Online community boards help people
connect to one another on shared interests. Geo-caching is a new activity enabled by
the Internet and Global Positioning System (GPS) devices, where people hide pack-
ages (caches) and list clues on the Internet. By searching out the clues and locations,
people engage in a high-tech treasure hunt and share their stories online.

Though some examples of DIY fun and play require engagement with the capitalist
system (you need a computer and a GPS device to geo-cache), many activities do not.
In short, there are a plethora of DIY entertainment options out there. Decolonizing
the world of play can be as easy as getting off the tour bus or getting online, or as
involved as starting a cooperative music venue.

Conclusion

These examples of do-it-yourself school, work, and play show the astounding array of
human behaviors that fall under the category of DIY. From the most important of
endeavors that humans undertake—how to raise and educate our offspring—to the
most light-hearted frivolities of entertainment, people engage in DIY behaviors on a
continuum from personal to political, individualist to collectivist, religious to secular.
From worker collectives to co-working spaces, from childcare cooperatives to home
schooling, people are moving away from relying on bosses, government, and professionals to do it themselves. Democratizing the workplace and firing your boss is one
thing, but can you also fire the government? Do-it-yourself government is the logical
next step from DIY work and school for some DIY lifestylers.

DISCUSSION QUESTIONS

1. Were you home schooled, or do you know someone who was? Are they DIY
   people? Are you suspicious of the public schools?
2. What are the challenges of a worker collective? What are the benefits of manag-
   ing ourselves instead of relying on a boss?
3. In what ways do you engage in DIY leisure? Do you use social networking websites to organize DIY play? Where would you go on a DIY vacation?

IV: Government and Media

S ocial theorists from Niccolò Machiavelli to Antonio Gramsci have commented on the need for consent from those who are governed. But what does this really mean? Has anyone recently asked if you agree with a 65 mph speed limit or whether corporations should be limited in campaign contributions? The laws that govern our everyday behavior rarely come down to a direct vote of the people. We live, instead, in a representative democracy where we elect people to do the work of governance. Presumably if we don't like what they are doing we elect someone else. But if we do not rise up and make our voices heard the authorities assume we consent to their laws.

Over the last 15 years there has been an upsurge in popular protest. Many social movement scholars noticed that the movements of the 1960s fizzled by the 1980s. But in the 1990s protests began to re-emerge, especially around issues of globalization. The protests in Seattle in November 1999 marked a new era of popular resistance to global governance. An estimated 100,000 union activists, radical anarchists, and just plain folks assembled in the Seattle rain outside the meetings of the World Trade Organization to protest expansion of transnational corporate powers (Smith 2001: 1; Smith and West 2005: 621).

The Seattle protests were remarkable in several ways. First, they showed the world that there was a new current of resistance, a movement that would gain energy through successive events around the world. But the protests in Seattle were not just a resurgence, they also brought about a new type of independent media where activists reported their own news from the front lines of the conflict. Known as **indymedia**, the Independent Media Center created in Seattle has been successfully reproduced in cities around the world, which continue to bring news and information to people via the Internet on indymedia.org.

One of the more remarkable outcomes of the new protest movements is the way they challenge notions of consent and resistance. Social and political theorists have long spoken of legitimate governance requiring the consent of the governed. If massive protests are happening on the streets, can we really describe a state of consent? And what is the mentality of being governed? This is a question that philosopher Michel Foucault began to investigate late in his career. His final books and lectures struggled with the changing face of power and how people come to accept the imposition of governance throughout their daily lives.

Figure 4.1 Protestors square off against police.
Source: Shutterstock

Foucault described the notion of "**governmentality**," or the manner in which people come to think about, and ultimately accept, outside authority governing their behaviors through both laws and moral socialization. Governmentality is a system of thought that goes without saying—it is something deeply ingrained in us that we do not question and might not even realize is there at all (Foucault 1994). But some people have questioned governmentality and the need for external authority. Instead of allowing elected officials and their enforcement agencies to govern us, some radical activists have decided to govern themselves. In common parlance the word "anarchy" is synonymous with chaos. But in social and political theory, the term anarchy means something quite different: it means self-organization.

DIY Government

Anarchism has a 150-year history as a political philosophy. Literally meaning "without rule," anarchism takes as a premise the rejection of all authority. It is a mode of social organization that is free from governance by religion, the market, or the state. Sometimes people use the slogan "no gods, no masters" to describe the fundamental philosophy of anarchism. But if anarchists reject the authority of others, who will keep order? They do it themselves.

Self-organization means there must be a strict notion of personal responsibility that can be generalized into moral principle. Far from being chaos, a self-organized DIY society would mean that people have to converse, agree, and consent to behaviors. DIY organization would mean there is no state, no boss, no religious authority, and no recognized leader or elected official. Such a community would entail "freedom from authority and rules; a place where people can live free from external compulsion. Thus police and even formalized laws would not be necessary" (O'Hara 1999: 95). But like governmentality, anarchism can also be a state of mind. Anarchy is not just an absence of laws but rather an absence of *the need* for the rule of law. Instead, people behave according to mutually accepted codes without the need for external coercion and enforcement powers.

How does anarchism work in action? Perhaps the best examples are anarchist communities where there is no need for government, police, or law. As well as some of the back-to-the-land examples discussed in Chapter II, there are intentional communities from Denmark to Colombia that operate without external or top-down authority. There are also "squats" across the world—temporarily inhabited spaces where squatters live illegally and unbeknownst to the owner. Usually these are uninhabited buildings, but they can also be camps in open spaces or vacant lots.

Christiania

In 1971 in Copenhagen, activists took over an abandoned military barracks and declared it "Freetown." Commonly known as Christiania due to its location in the Copenhagen borough of Christianshavn, over 40 years the population has grown to approximately 850 residents. Christiania was controversial from the start, but Danish residents grew to accept the community and its odd ways. Christiania was an experiment in self-organization from its inception—residents decide everything by consensus. They have firm rules, including a ban on stealing, violence, weapons, and hard drugs. These rules were developed by an agreement of all residents, and a similar agreement would be needed to alter the rules (Christiania 2004). According to its mission statement (Christiania 2011), Christiania is meant to be

> a self-governing society whereby each and every individual holds themselves responsible over the wellbeing of the entire community.

The principles of anarchism must be founded upon a strong basis of moral responsibility. The decolonization of the lifeworld means that we cannot rely on the authority of the police and government. The residents of Christiania have struggled with enforcing this—not among themselves but with outsiders. Over its long history, Christiania has become a destination for radical tourists who want to see anarchism in action, or perhaps just be free to do their own thing outside the bounds of state authorities. They want to experience a decolonized life.

Figure 4.2 Christiana, Denmark: "A city within a city for you and me."
Source: Shutterstock

This also attracts a certain amount of instability. The stance of the community has been to accept all-comers, including pensioners, single mothers, the homeless and mentally ill, and reforming addicts (Christiania 2004: 2):

> Among the local users are many social security recipients, pensioners, immigrants and clients from social institutions. Single mothers also visit here, not to mention the many homeless and jobless young people. Greenlanders, street people and vagabonds, all find a sanctuary here.

Of course this acceptance also means dealing with the consequences of diverse people expressing differing perspectives. Christiania has successfully dealt with such adversity, but not without difficulties. There have been violent attacks, a murder, and the controversial eviction of those who would not conduct themselves in a cooperative manner (Cablefish 2008).

But through these difficulties, Christiania persists. The residents have a collective industry designing and manufacturing utility bicycles. Cars are not allowed, and there is a common goal of economic sustainability (Christiania 2011):

> Our society is to be economically self-sustaining and, as such, our aspiration is to be steadfast in our conviction that psychological and physical destitution can be averted.

Residents of Christiania strive for fulfillment of broad human needs: psychological, physical, economic, and ecological. They feel that the rule of the state, religion, and other external authorities reduce the ability of people to achieve true fulfillment. They have developed their own community in a remarkably resilient 40-year-old example of DIY organization.

Gaviotas

In the northeastern plains of Colombia there is a small village of about 200 people called Gaviotas. This area of Colombia, known as the llanos, is a rugged desert where only grasses grow and rivers teem with malarial mosquitoes and piranhas. Very few people live in the llanos as it is rather inhospitable. The village was established in 1971 by a visionary named Paolo Lugari as an experimental solution to environmental and population problems (based in part on United Nations grant funding). Acknowledging the problems of the "green revolution" where agricultural technologies were exported from the west to the Global South, Lugari proposed to found a town in the hardest place rather than the easiest place, saying: "If we could do it there, we could do it anywhere. The only deserts are deserts of the imagination. Gaviotas is an oasis of imagination" (Weisman 1998a: 33). Lugari persuaded some of the best minds in Colombia to move 16 hours from Bogota to work on technological solutions appropriate to the area, and they were wildly successful: technology from Gaviotas has spread north to Central America and south to Chile.

What is most interesting about Gaviotas is not just environmental innovations, but also the self-organization of the community. Alan Weisman (1998b) describes a community that has no police or jail, no laws or rules: "housing, health care, and food are free here, and everyone earns the same above-minimum-wage salary." With no poverty, there's no crime. People respect socially agreed upon commonsense codes of conduct. The community ostracizes people who violate the protocol, and generally they leave for a place that is more socially comfortable. When asked about adultery or jealousy, community members responded that there is no marriage in Gaviotas. There is no church and no state to do the marrying, and so people just live together if they so desire. If relations change, people move on without the need for governmental or religious sanction: no gods, no masters.

This is DIY organization: like-minded people who agree on unwritten rules, living in cooperation without the need for laws or enforcement. Weisman describes cooperation in Gaviotas as "symphonic, each section adding its part without overpowering the rest" (Weisman 1998a: 156). In an exchange with a community member, Paulo Lugari suggests:

"We aren't communists. And we aren't a commune, either."
"What are we then? A company? A community?"
"Both. Neither. We're Gaviotas."

Lugari's words reflect the lack of models to describe DIY organization. There are few words or categories for such radical communities, which shows how deeply our minds have been colonized by the notions of governmentality—we have difficulty even describing what an alternative might look or feel like.

Itinerant Camps

Back in the Great Depression they were called jungle camps. Today, we just call them homeless encampments—if we notice them at all. But across the nation there are small communities of homeless men and women who band together for safety in numbers. These small groups, with revolving membership and a nomadic location, exist outside of mainstream society with few rules and only self-organization.

In Sacramento, within sight of the State Capitol building, a massive tent city arose in the open space between the American River and the Union Pacific railroad tracks in 2007 on almost the same ground as itinerant camps photographed by Dorothea Lange in 1936 (see Figure 4.3). This happens to be near my house, in an area where I walk my dog daily. I counted more than 200 tents and impromptu structures, indicating a population of perhaps several hundred people. This was but one camp—there were several spread around the city in various out-of-the-way locations. City officials encouraged homeless folks to move from downtown sidewalks to the tent cities, where the police and surrounding community largely ignored them—only occasionally would police harass occupants if goaded into action by local residents. Without government, there was open use of drugs, alcohol, prostitution, and, inevitably, squalor.

But the residents of tent city achieved something remarkable in their quest for stability. They built a self-organized community that policed itself. They called it Safe Ground, and they wrote a code of conduct and a pledge for inhabitants to agree to. Safe Ground was governed by a board of three elected elders who served a rotating one-month term. As one inhabitant told a reporter, "It comes from the bottom up, not the top down" (Vollmann 2011: 35).

These folks are truly outside of capitalism. While the residents of Christiania sell bicycles to the world, and Gaviotas started with grants from the United Nations,

Figure 4.3a Sacramento, California "tent city" 1936.
Source: Dorothea Lange, Courtesy Library of Congress

Figure 4.3b Sacramento, California "tent city" 2009.
Source: Author

these homeless lead a peripatetic life, moving from camp to camp, existing off the kindness of strangers such as volunteers from Food Not Bombs who cook free meals for all-comers. Many of them are mentally ill, struggling veterans, or recovering from addictions (or still feeding a habit). They have chosen to move outside the colonized lifeworld. The mobile Safe Ground camp represents their attempt to provide stability and security for themselves. This self-governance among the homeless is a necessary response to the threats of unhappy neighbors, police harassment, and internal threats from volatile members.

Squats

They sometimes call themselves travelers. They are punks, hippies, anarchists, or they fall outside categorization. They travel from place to place, sometimes hitchhiking, sometimes walking, often hopping a train. They live in jungle camps with the homeless or they cop a squat—intentionally inhabiting an unoccupied building without the permission of the owner. Squatters have been at it for a long time, sometimes taking decades to establish themselves in a permanent situation (Ferguson 2002).

Squatting can be a political statement or a necessity. Like the attempts to establish Safe Ground at homeless camps, there are politically motivated squatters who think of themselves as part of a movement to reclaim property from the capitalist ownership class. Sometimes called urban homesteading, such squatters will illegally live in empty housing in an attempt to upend traditional notions of property and human rights. In the recession of the last few years, squatters have multiplied greatly, taking over empty foreclosed houses (Peñalver 2009).

But squatting has a long history beyond urban homesteading. In major cities around the world people have occupied buildings for long periods, with a revolving population of locals and travelers. In New York City on Avenue C, "C-Squat" holds temporary and long-time residents. In describing the residents, journalist Sarah Ferguson says, "They're poets and carpenters, youth counselors and social workers, photographers and piercing artists, even a court clerk and a woman who works in the accounting department at MTV. There are also seniors, people with AIDS, former shelter residents, and just plain misfits who could never afford anywhere else to live" (Ferguson 2002). C-Squat residents have a sense of community and appreciation for the space and each other. Ferguson interviewed an elder of the squat who said: "Kids with no family created family here. We rehabbed the building, and the building rehabbed us" (Ferguson 2002). Living the DIY lifestyle, the residents have contributed to the surrounding community by starting community gardens and food cooperatives.

Permanent squats often have rules and structures for behavior, generally arrived at through consensus decision-making processes. DIY organization in the more permanent squats can involve a cadre of longer-term residents who are given deference and may at times become something like authority. As one squatter told me:

Figure 4.4 An abandoned foreclosed home.
Source: Shutterstock

> Most of the well-established squats I've been to have rules, and a lot have full-time residents who make up the "authority."

DIY organization usually means consensus among the entire community, but in some cases it can be a smaller group of trusted full-time and long-term squatters who more or less run the show. Less permanent squats have different issues to deal with, the first of which being how to find them.

Travelers often have a network they rely on to find a squat in a new and unfamiliar area. People exchange names in squats as they travel, and keep in touch by sending messages with other travelers or by email and social network Internet sites. Travelers also engage in community work and advocacy, so the social networks link up across cities and nations, and people in one place tend to know about other places. Squats often have communal food, and squatters will work with local Food Not Bombs or similar groups—information is exchanged during meal preparation about good places to visit. Many traveling squatters were hesitant to speak with me (an outsider), but the few who felt comfortable suggested that notions of community and identity are central to making self-government work in a squat, and that often times you know who can give you good information just by looking at them:

> Sometimes we'd get to a place and look for people who "looked like us." That means dreads, piercings, a certain style of clothing. That doesn't really work as

well anymore, since you can get piercings at the mall now, and holes in your face no longer tend to correlate with political views. But we'd find them, and they'd take us home.

What "home" looks like is another matter, and it varies quite a bit from place to place. Some squats are homey and well-maintained, others are dilapidated and filthy. Like the more permanent squats, there are a few common-sense rules. If there is too much noise, or the occupation of the property is too obvious, neighbors might alert the authorities. The most obvious of rules, then, is to keep the noise down and not draw attention to one's self. But as one traveler told me:

> Even in the more loosely organized squats, there were a lot of places that didn't allow meat, drugs, or (overt) sexism/homophobia/racism.

In other words, squats are intended to be open, inclusive communities where people can be free, while not oppressing others. Similar in politics to the music venue 924 Gilman and the punk rock community, this can be a delicate balance and part of the main problem with self-organization.

How does one do DIY government? If the goal of a group is to free themselves from political, economic, or general authority (no gods, no masters), then what keeps them from alternately devolving into true chaos or letting "might" make "right"? Part of the answer is consensus decision-making, and another part is the moral rectitude discussed above. But part of the answer involves Foucault's notion of governmentality. Once you free yourself from the mindset of being governed and open up to the idea that we should govern ourselves, many difficulties disappear. Like-minded people agree to live together in a squat, and if you are not of a like mind you don't live there. Anarchism means not needing rules or policing. In this sense, anarchism is more a state of mind than a political theory. It is a way of thinking in which being free from the authority of the boss, police, and experts means living a life of doing it yourself.

Overall, squatters tend towards being DIY in many ways throughout their lives, so they can be classified as DIY lifestylers. As one squatter told me:

> I would like to be a DIY person, and I think squatting helped me believe that I could do things on my own. I know how to turn the water off and on at the street so I can fix the plumbing … we helped fix a 150-year old slate roof on a squat in London. … I think a lot of it has to do with not having money, too—if you can't afford a plumber or roofer, you do it yourself.

In other words, travelers in squats learn do-it-yourself skills that they can apply throughout their lives. While somewhat motivated by financial necessity, squatters are also motivated by the desire to travel, the wish to be free from authority, and to follow their passions. As one traveler told me:

I think of myself as part of an amorphous community that is trying to help each other out and create greater opportunities to follow our passions. We are trying to do it ourselves and do it together.

The "squattercity" blogger Robert Neuwirth (http://squattercity.blogspot.com/) embodies the DIY attitude in most of what he does: by publishing his own writing about people who are governing themselves in their own communities he demonstrates the DIY lifestyle. Bloggers are part of the new wave of do-it-yourself media.

DIY Media

Many people spanning the political spectrum find the mainstream media suspect. Those on the political left find an overriding bias in the profit motive and interests of the massive corporations that own the main outlets of information. Those on the political right suspect a liberal bias on the part of reporters. The response among some is to buy their own news outlet: Roger Ailes reportedly approached Rupert Murdoch about funding Fox News because he found CNN to be "too liberal" (Auletta 2003: 61). But for those of us who do not have personal fortunes capable of financing a new 24-hour cable news network, there is an alternative. The 1999 Seattle protests discussed above brought a new form of news to the world: DIY media. The indymedia organizations around the world are a testament to the rise of the DIY movement using new technology and information-gathering techniques. Nowhere is this more clearly demonstrated than with the birth of the blogosphere.

What we now call "blogs" started out in the late 1990s as a way of cataloging information on the World Wide Web: a web log. This term was first combined into weblog and then shortened to "blogs" (Blood 2000). Though they can also be worst-case examples of narcissism (*The Economist* magazine reports that the average blog has just seven readers), blogs now represent the cutting edge of DIY media. They allow individuals to post material to a website in reverse-chronological order, with the latest news up top and archives going back as long as desired. The popularity of blogs has grown astronomically—there is even a blog to measure blogs: what numbered in the thousands in 1999 grew to 162 million by May 2011 (Blogpulse 2011; Blood 2000).

Judged simply from sheer numbers, blogs represent the democratization of the Internet. While some may call this vanity, others call it the most full expression of freedom of speech. Yet critics have called blogs "the toilet walls of the internet" and rhetorically asked: "What on earth gives every computer-owner the right to express his opinion, unasked for?" (*Economist* Staff Writer 2006). Of course the answer is contained within the question itself: as the number of computer owners and users grows, so too does their ability to engage in digitized free speech.

Blogs are a way to share all kinds of information, from news, to political views, to recipes, to what you had for breakfast. Most interesting from the DIY perspective are the ways that blogs have become platforms for learning about how to do things yourself and connecting to other DIYers. As one blogger put it, "What really excited me was that I got to design the thing myself, choose its name, code it, write it, and then publish it without anyone else" (Rosenberg 2009: 229).

Ree Drummond, who blogs as "The Pioneer Woman," is a classic example of the DIY lifestyler. She got interested in blogs after getting married and moving back to a ranch in Oklahoma (she had moved to Los Angeles to pursue college and then broadcast journalism). She was researching how to home school her children, and ended up creating a blog that has 23.3 million page views by 4.4 million unique visitors per month, 95 percent of which, Drummond estimates, are female. Turning the blog first into a best-selling cookbook and now a best-selling memoir, *From Black Heels to Tractor Wheels* (optioned for a movie starring Reese Witherspoon), Drummond has captured a certain star power for the DIY movement (Fortini 2011).

The Pioneer Woman blog is separated into several categories (Drummond 2011):

> In my Cooking section, I post step-by-step photos of all the cowboy-friendly dishes I've taught myself to cook through the years. … In the Home & Garden section, I show the step-by-step saga of a start-to-finish remodeling project of an old guest house on our ranch … And in the Homeschooling section, I discuss the adventure of homeschooling four children on an isolated cattle ranch.

Figure 4.5 Two cows on Ree Drummond's ranch.
Source: pioneerwomen.com

In other words, Ree Drummond is a DIY lifestyler. She lives on a working ranch, grows and processes her own food, home schools her children, and blogs about all of it.

Blogs are one form of what is known to Internet insiders as user-generated content (UGC) and sometimes referenced as the second life of the Internet, or Web 2.0. According to the Pew Internet and American Life Project, 35 percent of adults and 57 percent of teenagers post their own content (Lenhart 2006). By far the largest use of bandwidth are homemade videos on **YouTube**, with 100 million videos watched each day, constituting 60 percent of videos on the Internet (Cheng, Dale, and Liu 2008: 229; Gill et al. 2007: 15).

Established in 2005 (and purchased by Google in 2006), YouTube provides download-as-you-watch video, with content coming from established television, film, and music video producers as well as the user-generated content promised by the website's tagline "Broadcast Yourself" (YouTube 2011). As I write this, the most popular video on YouTube is Justin Bieber's music video "Baby," which has half a billion views (Van Buskirk 2011). As such, YouTube is just another vehicle for old forms of media, albeit on a new platform.

But one thing that makes YouTube different from other video and UGC sites is the social networking aspects: users can rate and comment upon videos, and similar videos are suggested to viewers by an internal algorithm. This allows popular videos to rise organically by viewer ratings, and videos and viewers can connect. YouTube organizes this massive amount of content by offering categories such as recently featured, most viewed, top rated, and most discussed (Cheng, Dale, and Liu 2008: 230). This "crowd sourcing" or "collective intelligence" appeals to our mythological notions of democracy: if it is that popular, it *must* be good—or at least worth a look. Of course, with 75 billion videos online, one must question if there is a trade of quantity for quality. Andrew Keen, in his polemic about digital culture, argued that "YouTube eclipses even the blogs in the inanity and absurdity of its content" and "the monkeys" are now "running the show" (2007: 5, 9).

YouTube's user-generated content represents an almost unlimited source of DIY creativity. Anyone with a digital camera can produce it (and cameras are built in to many computers and most smart phones today), and anyone with access to the Internet can view it. It is direct and immediate, there is no institutional or market mediation. YouTube thus represents a decolonization (in Habermas's sense) of popular culture. When content is produced by amateurs and viewed by amateurs, experts and profits are left out of the loop. Capitalism's only ability to turn a profit in this system is by showing advertisements from the distribution platform, and YouTube still hasn't turned a profit (*Economist* Staff Writer 2011).

YouTube thus represents a new form of **popular culture**. Since the advent of radio, through the age of television and into the Internet era, social critics have argued that popular culture (mass production for mass consumption) has a flattening effect on consumers. Popular culture undermines traditional folk cultures and remakes them into consumable, profit-orientated commodities (Adorno 1991; Jenkins 2008; Kellner 1995; Marcuse 1964). Thus "folks playing music" on a back porch somewhere becomes a "folk music" category in the music store. But YouTube upends this colonization of art. User-generated content can become wildly popular by "going viral" (to use Internet parlance). This brings creativity from the people to the people without being mediated by the record companies or film studios (though it is mediated by YouTube as an information portal). And so, YouTube can be seen as a disruptive technology (Burgess and Green 2009).

But it's not quite this simple. (Is it ever?) There are numerous success stories where content goes viral and ordinary people's creativity is discovered. These people get slotted into the corporate, commodity-driven system of popular culture. To "make it" still means to land a contract with a major production company. So just as reality TV purports to democratize the old tube by showing us real people, YouTube may disrupt an old system by showing us content made by ordinary folks—but it might also reasonably be seen as a way to deliver new talent to the pop culture machine, just as stars from American Idol are delivered to the major recording labels.

Before the term "blog" was even coined in 1997, one of the earliest blogs called itself an online 'zine. A 'zine is a homemade, self-published magazine. Combining self-written essays with cut-and-pasted text, 'zines are then photocopied and distributed hand-to-hand or by mail. 'Zines represent one of the first efforts at DIY media, taking a technology (copy machines) and re-purposing it to fight the mainstream media. Classic 'zines include *Cometbus* and *Maximum RocknRoll*, both of which were involved with founding 924 Gilman. 'Zines aren't just about punk rock, though. They might discuss any number of issues relevant to the producer and her audience. One issue of *Cometbus* (2005), for example, published interviews and recollections from people who had grown up on communes, and what it was like to move into mainstream society after a DIY youth (see Figure 4.6). There's even a 'zine called *Complete Manual for Pirate Radio*, which is another example of re-purposing older technology.

Of course amateur radio operators (or ham radio) have been around for a long time. But the invention and marketing of relatively inexpensive micro-transmitters has given life to a new breed of radio operators and disc jockeys who use the interstices of the radio spectrum to broadcast their message to local listeners. Extremely local, in fact: many pirate radio stations, or "free radio" as some prefer to call them, can be heard only in the vicinity of a few square blocks. Pirate radio is an example of people taking control of a government-regulated media and turning it to their own ends, which in fact are often anti-governmental, because many free radio stations are explicitly anarchist in their perspective. This is DIY media in a much more intensive way than broadcasting yourself through YouTube or writing a blog. Pirate radio, since it is illegal, can put operators at risk for prosecution by the authorities.

Figure 4.6 Cometbus 'zine 2005.

Conclusion

Do-it-yourself government and media are not obvious forms of the DIY movement. Most people don't know that squats and pirate radio stations exist—and those involved usually want to keep things that way. Most people have little to no interest in the majority of blogs or 'zines, and most videos on YouTube are watched by only a handful of people. But for those who live a DIY lifestyle and take on the identity of a squatter, an anarchist, or a blogger, nothing could be more central. This is a lifestyle that can define who people are, how they interact, and how they present themselves to the public. But as history moves forward and subcultural styles are coopted and sold in the mall, these identities become simultaneously more available to everyone and less meaningful in their message. Certain styles of presentation no longer convey particular political or social stances, they no longer indicate that someone is interested in DIY governance.

DIY governance can be thought of as a state of mind. Michel Foucault suggested that we have a mindset of "governmentality"; we consent to be governed, directed, and regulated. Some people chafe at this perceived lack of freedom. They wish instead to govern themselves, or as the anarchist slogan says: "There's no government like no government." Shaking off the mindset of governmentality is so difficult as to be perhaps impossible. But some people in the corners of the DIY movement are making a valiant attempt.

DISCUSSION QUESTIONS

1. How do we follow rules without thinking about them? Recall a time when you were acting in accordance with authority without realizing it. What would you change about this?
2. Do you trust the mainstream media? Why, or why not? Do some outlets seem more responsible than others? Would you trust independent journalists more than professionals?
3. Do you think anarchism could work on a larger scale than the small, like-minded communities discussed here? What would have to change for this to work in your neighborhood, city, or county?

V: Conclusion

The Search for Control

~∗~

Control eludes many of us in the modern moment. We rely on others for much of our lives: the bosses and assistants at work, elected officials and their staff in our government, farmers and clerks in the supermarket for our food, and teachers for our education. We are all searching for control, and some of us find fulfillment in the many realms of social behavior that fall under the category of DIY. By doing things ourselves we move outside the realm of normal—at least normal for today. But what isn't customary today was common in years past. Sometimes this can be uncomfortable, but it can also be liberating and empowering.

Today there are many parts of our lives that are accelerated beyond our comfort level. Some forms of acceleration are fun and exhilarating: the rush of the ski slope, the throaty roar of a powerful automobile, or the risk-laden edginess of skydiving. But these moments of acceleration are just examples of our search for authentic emotion. We search for realness because we have a nagging sense that something important is missing. Whether we realize it or not, by seeking out dramatic entertainment we seek meaning, identity, and rootedness in a world teeming with pretense.

Finding a niche of authenticity and fulfillment has perhaps always been a struggle. Some embrace the information flow and dive headlong into blogs and YouTube. Others are less comfortable with a life lived in ones and zeros and instead retreat from the grid to grow their own food and govern their own conduct. Even in these opposing responses people are doing it themselves. At its best, DIY means that people are connecting the micro and macro levels of their lives using what C. Wright Mills called the *sociological imagination* (Mills 1959). DIYers are using their sociological imaginations to find a solution to alienation, mystification, and loss of control. They are moving back to the land, schooling their own children, and governing themselves. In short, people are taking back their daily lives from systems that are otherwise beyond their individual control. They are freeing themselves from the abstract and impersonal forces of money, power, and bureaucracy.

The DIY movement represents a shift away from relying on experts and professionals towards self-reliance and independence from the larger systems of governance and capitalism—what Habermas called the decolonization of the lifeworld. This is a take back, whether politically or financially motivated. But the adversary is strong:

capitalists and bureaucrats have found ways to coopt or stall the DIY movement, offering DIY-lite goods and services or putting up barriers like building or health codes. Recolonization of that which DIY seeks to decolonize is always at hand, and we can see it for sale at Home Depot, we can watch it on the DIY network, and no doubt there is a blog about it somewhere.

The past and present of DIY are fairly clear—people have been doing it themselves for a long time, and continue to do so today in many ways and for a variety of reasons. Sometimes people are doing it themselves due to political beliefs, and others for simple economic reasons. Not everyone owns a house and can farm their backyard. Even fewer can move back to the land or create a commune. But almost one-quarter of U.S. households have a vegetable garden. Millions of Americans fix up their own houses, preserve their own food, and enjoy crafting in their spare time. Some of the more entrepreneurial of us even make a living at it.

But what is the future of DIY? If the environmentalists are right and capitalism is fundamentally unsustainable—if our natural resources like oil, timber, fresh water, and clean air are fundamentally scarce—then DIY might not just be a personal choice. It might be a necessity. Perhaps it will be the peaking of oil that causes rampant inflation. It might be the over-tapped fresh water supplies in places as different as California and Palestine that tips the scales. Maybe it will be an economic bubble bursting in the markets of a world super-power fighting two or three wars at once. Maybe a catastrophe will add to the mix—an earthquake and tsunami or a deep-water oilrig explosion. It doesn't take a cranky pessimist to imagine a world in the not-too-distant future where everything that we now take comfort in disappears quickly. Under such a future scenario, doing it yourself may no longer be a personal decision; it might be the key to a sustainable future. It is entirely possible that the 21st century will move leaps and bounds from present technologies—just not in the expected direction of "progress," but instead towards the pre-capitalist and ecologically sustainable recent past where people lived off what they could grow, educated their own children, and governed themselves as they saw fit.

In 1929 Antonio Gramsci, imprisoned by Mussolini's fascist government, wrote in a letter from prison that we must have "pessimism of the intellect, but optimism of the will" (Gramsci 1971: 175). If we examine the world with our intellect we may come to disheartening conclusions. But these conclusions don't sit well with us because we desire a better future, we have an optimism that spurs us on to take action in the world and in our daily lives even though it may feel intellectually hopeless at times. And this involves many little actions and behavioral changes that can make a difference—if only to us and those in our immediate circle of influence. This might mean taking yourself off the grid, or growing your own food, or a million little things that may not mean much in the grand scheme of things, but matter in our lives. The optimism that we hew towards, this will for something better, is what can change the world. Sometimes social change happens through big revolutions and grand historical events.

But social change also happens through the aggregated millions of little alterations at the individual level. When we do it ourselves—when we reject reliance on others and take control of our own lives—we are enacting radical social change. In DIY we can find the seeds of change, but of course we also see the recolonization by the forces of money and power. It is up to us all to wage this struggle for control and self-reliance.

DISCUSSION QUESTIONS

1. Do you feel a lack of control in your life? What forces drive your behaviors towards inauthenticity? How might you counteract these forces?
2. When you do things for yourself, without experts, do you feel a closer connection to what you achieve?
3. Do you have pessimism of the intellect and/or optimism of the will? When you look at the world around you, do you see things that could be improved by people taking DIY action?

References

Adorno, Theodor. 1991. *The Culture Industry.* New York: Routledge.

Agnew, Eleanor. 2004. *Back from the Land.* Lanham, MA: Ivan R. Dee.

Auletta, Ken. 2003. "Vox Fox." *The New Yorker* (May 26): 58–73.

Aurini, Janice, and Scott Davies. 2005. "Choice without Markets: Homeschooling in the Context of Private Education." *British Journal of Sociology of Education 26*(4): 461–74.

Barlow, Aaron. 2008. *Blogging America.* Westport, CT: Praeger.

Berger, Bennett M. 1981. *The Survival of a Counterculture.* Berkeley: University of California Press.

Blacker, David. 1998. "Fanaticism and Schooling in the Democratic State." *American Journal of Education 106*(2): 241–72.

Blogpulse. 2011. "Blogpulse stats." Retrieved May 16, 2011 (http://www.blogpulse.com/).

Blood, Rebecca. 2000. "Weblogs: A History and Perspective." *Rebecca's Pocket.* Retrieved September 7, 2000 (http://www.rebeccablood.net/essays/weblog_history.html).

Blumer, Herbert. 1969. "Social Movements." Pp. 8–29 in *Studies in Social Movements,* ed. B. McLaughlin. New York: Free Press.

Bowles, Samuel, and Herbert Gintis. 1976. *Schooling in Capitalist America.* New York: Basic Books.

Burgess, Kean, and Joshua Green. 2009. *YouTube: Online Video and Participatory Culture.* Cambridge, UK: Polity.

Cablefish. 2008. "Christiania Fires It Up." *Indymedia UK.* Retrieved October 29, 2008 (http://www.indymedia.org.uk/en/2008/10/411883.html).

Cheng, Xu, Cameron Dale, and Jiangchuan Liu. 2008. "Statistics and Social Network of YouTube Videos." 16th International Workshop of Quality of Service.

Christiania. 2004. *The Christiania Guide.* Retrieved May 1, 2011 (http://www.christiania.org/inc/guide/?lan=gb&side=1).

Christiania. 2011. *The Christiania Facebook Page* (a partial reconstruction of the 1971 Mission Statement). Retrieved May 1, 2011 (http://www.facebook.com/group.php?gid=138170166227676).

Cometbus, Aaron. 2005. *Cometbus.* 'Zine #48.

Conkin, Paul K. 1967. *The New Deal.* New York: Thomas Y. Crowell Company.

Co-working Wiki. 2011. Retrieved March 1, 2011 (http://wiki.coworking.info/w/page/16583831/FrontPage).

Craig, Ben, and John Pencavel. 1992. "The Plywood Companies of the Pacific Northwest." *The American Economic Review 82*(5): 1083–105.

Cupid Courier Collective. 2011. Retrieved May 1, 2011 (http://www.cupidcourier.com/).

Curl, John. 2009. *For All the People*. Oakland: PM Press.

Drummond, Ree. 2011. "The Pioneer Woman." Retrieved May 16, 2011 (http://thepioneerwoman.com/about/).

Economist Staff Writer. 2006. "It's the Links, Stupid: Blogging is Just Another Word for Having Conversations." *The Economist* (April 20). Retrieved April 20, 2006 (http://www.economist.com/node/6794172).

Economist Staff Writer. 2011. "From Cash Cow to Cachet: The Fall and Rise of The Music Video." *The Economist* (January 6). Retrieved January 6, 2011 (http://www.economist.com/node/17857409).

Edge, Brian, ed. 2004. *924 Gilman: The Story So Far … .* Oakland: AK Press.

Ellerman, David. 1984. "Workers' Cooperatives: The Question of Legal Structure." Pp. 257–73 in *Worker Cooperatives in America*, eds. Robert Jackall and Henry M. Levin. Berkeley: University of California Press.

Emerson, Ralph Waldo. 2010 [1841]. "Self Reliance." In *Ralph Waldo Emerson: The First and Second Series*. Washington, D.C.: Library of America.

Etsy. 2010. Retrieved November 2010 (www.etsy.com/about).

Farris, Michael, and Scott A. Woodruff. 2000. "The Future of Home Schooling." *Peabody Journal of Education* 75(½): 233–55.

Ferguson, Sarah. 2002. "Better Homes and Squatters: New York's Outlaw Homesteaders Earn the Right to Stay." *The Village Voice* (August 27). Retrieved August 27, 2002 (http://www.villagevoice.com/2002-08-27/news/better-homes-and-squatters/1/).

Fish, Corrina. 2011. "This Land is Your Land, This Land is My Land: Looking Back at 50 Years of the Capitol Area Plan." *The Sacramento Press* (January 31). Retrieved January 31, 2011 (http://www.sacramentopress.com/headline/44690).

Fortini, Amanda. 2011. "O Pioneer Woman." *The New Yorker* (May 9): 26–31.

Foucault, Michel. 1994. "Governmentality." Pp. 201–22 in *Power*, ed. James B. Faubion. Volume 3 of *The Essential Works of Michel Foucault 1954–1984*, series ed. Paul Rabinow. New York: The New Press.

Francis, Mark. 1987. "Some Different Meanings Attached to a City Park and Community Gardens." *Landscape Journal* 6(2): 101–12.

Gallagher Group. 2007. *Examining the Impact of Food Deserts on Public Health in Detroit*. Chicago: 2007 Mari Gallagher Research & Consulting Group.

Gatto, John Taylor. 2003. "Against School." *Harper's Magazine* (September): 33–38.

Gill, Phillipa, Martin Arlitt, Zongpeng Li, and Anirban Mahanti. 2007. "YouTube Traffic Characterization: A View from the Edge." *Proceedings of the 7th ACM SIGCOMM Conference on Internet Measurement*. New York: ACM.

Gladwell, Malcolm. 2009. "Priced to Sell." *The New Yorker* (July 6): 80–84.

Gould, Peter C. 1988. *Early Green Politics*. New York: St. Martin's Press.

Gramsci, Antonio. 1971. *Selections from the Prison Notebooks*. Edited and translated by Quintin Hoare and Geoffrey Nowell Smith. New York: International Publishers.

Greenberg, Edward S. 1984. "Producer Cooperatives and Democratic Theory: The Case of the Plywood Firms." Pp. 171–213 in *Worker Cooperatives in America*, eds. Robert Jackall and Henry M. Levin. Berkeley: University of California Press.

Guthrie, Woody. 1941. *The Columbia River Recordings*. Produced by Moe Asch. Smithsonian Folkways.

Habermas, Jurgen. 1984. *The Theory of Communicative Action*. Translated by Thomas McCarthy. Boston: Beacon Press.

Home Depot, The. 2010. *Annual Report*. The Home Depot: Atlanta.

Houston, Robert G. Jr., and Eugenia F. Toma. 2003. "Home Schooling: An Alternative School Choice." *Southern Economic Journal 69*(4): 920–35.

Independent Media Center (IMC). 2011. Retrieved May 1, 2011 (www.indymedia.org).

Jackall, Robert. 1984. "Paradoxes of Collective Work: A Study of the Cheeseboard, Berkeley, California." Pp. 109–35 in *Worker Cooperatives in America*, eds. Robert Jackall and Henry M. Levin. Berkeley: University of California Press.

Jackall, Robert, and Henry M. Levin (Eds.). 1984. *Worker Cooperatives in America*. Berkeley: University of California Press.

Jenkins, Henry. 2008. *Convergence Culture*. New York: NYU Press.

Johnson, Ana Gutierrez, and William Foote Whyte. 1977. "The Mondragón System of Worker Production Cooperatives." *Industrial and Labor Relations Review 31*(1): 18–30.

Jones, Derek C. 1984. "American Producer Cooperatives and Employee-Owned Firms: A Historical Perspective." In *Worker Cooperatives in America*, eds. Robert Jackall and Henry M. Levin. Berkeley: University of California Press.

Karabel, Jeremy, and A. H. Halsey, eds. 1977. *Power and Ideology in Education*. New York: Oxford University Press.

Kasmir, Sharryn, 1996. *The Myth of Mondragón*. Albany: State University of New York Press.

Keen, Andrew. 2007. *The Cult of the Amateur*. New York: Doubleday/Currency.

Kellner, Douglas. 1995. *Media Culture*. New York: Routledge.

Kingsolver, Barbara (with Steven L. Hopp and Camille Kingsolver). 2007. *Animal, Vegetable, Miracle*. New York: Harper Collins.

Klein, Joe. 1980. *Woody Guthrie: A Life*. New York: Ballantine Books.

lavaca collective, the. 2007. *Sin Patron*. [Translated by Katherine Kohlstedt]. Chicago: Haymarket Books.

Lee, Jenny, and Paul Abowd. 2011. "Detroit's Grassroots Economies." *In These Times*. Retrieved March 17, 2011 (http://inthesetimes.com/article/7089/detroits_grassroots_economies).

Lenhart, Amanda. 2006. "User-Generated Content." *Pew Internet and American Life Project*. Retrieved November 6, 2006 (http://www.pewinternet.org/Presentations/2006/UserGenerated-Content. aspx).

Lines, Patricia M. 2000. "Homeschooling Comes of Age." *The Public Interest* 140 (Summer 2000): 74–85.

Live Nude Girls Unite! 2000. Documentary film directed by Vicky Funari and Julia Query. Released by First Run/Icarus Films.

Lowe's Companies, Inc. 2009. *Annual Report*. Mooresville NC: Lowe's.

Lusty Lady. 2011. (http://www.lustyladysf.com/history/)

McDowell, Susan A., Annette R. Sanchez, and Susan S. Jones. 2000. "Participation and Perception: Looking at Home Schooling through a Multicultural Lens." *Peabody Journal of Education* 75(½): 124–46.

MacLeod, Greg. 1997. *From Mondragón to America*. Sydney, Nova Scotia: University College of Cape Breton Press.

Maker Faire. 2010. "FAQ." Retrieved May 1, 2011 (http://makerfaire.com/).

Manning, Richard. 2004. "The Oil We Eat." *Harper's Magazine* (February).

Marcuse, Herbert. 1964. *One Dimensional Man*. Boston: Basic Books.

Marsh, Jan. 1982. *Back to the Land*. London: Quartet Books.

Marx, Karl. 1967 [1867]. *Capital*. New York: International Publishers.

Maybeck High School. 2011. Retrieved May 1, 2011 (http://www.maybeckhs.org/home.html).

Mencken, H. L. 1924. "The Library." *American Mercury Magazine* Vol. 1: 504–7.

Mills, C. Wright. 1959. *The Sociological Imagination*. Oxford: Oxford University Press.

Morrison, Roy. 1991. *We Build the Road as We Travel*. Philadelphia: New Society Publishers.

Neuwirth, Robert. 2011. "Squattercity: Squatters and Squatter Cities Around the World." Retrieved May 1, 2011 (http://squattercity.blogspot.com/).

O'Hara, Craig. 1999. *The Philosophy of Punk*. San Francisco: AK Press.

Pallo, Erica. 2011. "SF Underground Market: A Little Bit Legal and a Whole Lotta Fantastic!" *Caliber Magazine* (6 March).

Peñalver, Eduardo M. 2009. "Homesteaders in the Hood." *Slate* (25 March).

Ray, Brian D. 1997. *Strengths of Their Own: Homeschoolers across America*. Salem: National Home Education Research Institute.

Romanowski, Michael H. 2001. "Common Arguments about the Strengths and Limitations of Home Schooling." *The Clearing House* 75(2): 79–83.

Rosenberg, Scott. 2009. *Say Everything*. New York: Crown Publishing.

Roszak, Theodore. 1969. *The Making of a Counter Culture*. Garden City, NY: Doubleday.

Sedaris, Amy. 2010. *Simple Times: Crafts for Poor People*. New York: Grand Central Publishing.

Smith, Jackie. 2001. "Globalizing Resistance: The Battle of Seattle and the Future of Social Movements." *Mobilization* 6(1): 1–19.

Smith, Jackie, and Dawn West. 2005. "The Uneven Geography of Global Civil Society: National and Global Influences on Transnational Association." *Social Forces* 84(2): 621–52.

Szasz, Andrew. 2007. *Shopping Our Way to Safety*. Minneapolis: University of Minnesota Press.

The Take. 2004. Documentary film directed by Avi Lewis and Naomi Klein. Released by First Run Features/Icarus Films.

Thomas, Henk, and Chris Logan. 1982. *Mondragón*. London: George Allen and Unwin.

Thoreau, Henry David. 1953 [1854]. *Walden*. New York: Mentor Books.

Thoreau, Henry David. 2007 [1862]. *Walking*. Rockville, Maryland: ARC Manor.

United States Census Bureau. 2000. "Quick Facts." Retrieved May 1, 2011 (http://quickfacts.census.gov/qfd/states/26/2622000.html).

United States Census Bureau. 2009. "Annual Estimates of the Resident Population for Incorporated Places Over 100,000." Retrieved May 1, 2011 (http://www.census.gov/popest/cities/SUB-EST 2009.html).

United States Census Bureau. 2010. "Table 1205." *Statistical Abstract of the United States*. Retrieved May 1, 2011 (http://www.census.gov/compendia/statab/2010/tables/10s1205.pdf).

Urban Farming Guys. 2011. Retrieved March 1, 2011 (http://www.hantzfarmsdetroit.com).

Urban Hive. 2011. Retrieved March 1, 2011 (http://theurbanhive.squarespace.com/).

Van Buskirk, Eliot. 2011. "Free Music Can Pay as Well as Paid Music, YouTube Says." *Wired Magazine* Epicenter Blog. Retrieved February 2, 2011 (http://www.wired.com/epicenter/2011/02/free-music-can-pay/all/1).

Varano, Charles S. 1999. *Forced Choices*. Albany: State University of New York Press.

Vollmann, William T. 2011. "Homeless in Sacramento." *Harper's Magazine 322*(1930): 28–46.

Webb, Pamela. 1983. "By the Sweat of the Brow: The Back-to-the-Land Movement in Depression Arkansas." *The Arkansas Historical Quarterly 42*(4): 332–45.

Wehr, Kevin. 2009. *Hermes on Two Wheels: The Sociology of Bicycle Messengers*. New York: University Press of America.

Weisman, Alan. 1998a. *Gaviotas*. White River Junction, VT: Chelsea Green Publishing.

Weisman, Alan. 1998b. "Gaviotas, Colombia: A Radio Documentary." *Living on Earth*. Somerville, MA: Public Radio International.

White, Richard. 1980. "Poor Men on Poor Lands: The Back-to-the-Land Movement of the Early Twentieth Century: A Case Study." *Pacific Historical Review 49*(1): 105–31.

Whyte, William Foote. 1982. "Social Inventions for Solving Human Problems." *American Sociological Review 47*(1): 1–13.

Whyte, William Foote, and Kathleen King Whyte. 1988. *Making Mondragón*. Ithaca: ILR Press New York School of Industrial and Labor Relations, Cornell University.

Woofter, T. J. Jr. 1936. "Rural Relief and the Back-to-the-Farm Movement." *Social Forces 14*(3): 382–88.

Worster, Donald. 1979. *Dust Bowl*. Oxford: Oxford University Press.

Yablonski, Lewis. 1968. *The Hippie Trip*. New York: Pegasus.

YouTube. 2011. *About YouTube*. Retrieved May 1, 2011 (http://www.youtube.com/t/about_youtube).

Zinn, Howard. 1999. *A People's History of the United States, 1492–Present*. New York: Perennial Classics.

Glossary/Index

A

Abowd, Paul 8, 18

Adorno, Theodore 54

Agnew, Eleanor 15

Ailes, Roger 51

alienation: Karl Marx's term for the separation of a worker from her product and the life force that went into making that product (associated with mystification and capitalism) 6–7

amateur radio operators 54

American Dream 12, 21

anarchism: literally "without rule," a political theory of self-organization 42–43, 50

Animal, Vegetable, Miracle 16

Argentinian worker-run factories 36

Auletta, Ken 51

Aurini, Janice 29

authenticity 10, 57

B

back to the land: a social movement where people move from the city to the countryside, usually to live more simply and closer to nature 6, 11–21

backyard gardeners 19–20

barriers to DIY 8–9, 20, 57–58

Berger, Bennett 15

Berkeley cooperative supermarket 36

bicycle messenger cooperative 34

biodiesel 27

Blacker, David 28

blog: a website where the newest content is listed first, generally authored by ordinary people, intended for a wide audience 4, 51–53, 54

Blogpulse 51

Blood, Rebecca 51
Blumer, Herbert 4
Bowles, Samuel 28

C

Cablefish 44

canning 20

capitalism: an economic system where productive capacity is privately owned and
run for the benefit of the owners (contrast to communism) 6–7, 8, 58
cooption of DIY movement 25, 26
and DIY media 53
and leisure time 38–39
public schools meeting needs of 33

casual carpools 27

Cheng, Xu 53

childcare groups 27

Christiania 43–45

code enforcement 8–9, 20

colonization of the lifeworld: a term used by Jurgen Habermas to describe the way
that money and power invade our personal lives 8, 19, 21, 38–39, 46

Cometbus 54, 55

communes: collectively run intentional communities, where back-to-the-landers
might settle 15–16

community gardens 16–19, 48

Community Supported Agriculture (CSA) 16

Conkin, Paul 12

control, search for 9–10, 57–59

co-working 33–34

crafters, DIY 23–25

Craig, Ben 35

Craigslist 39–40

"C-Squat," New York 48

Cupid Courier Collective, San Francisco 34

Curl, John 35, 36

D

Dale, Cameron 53

Davies, Scott 29

decolonization of the lifeworld: behavior that removes the influence of money and
power from our personal lives 8, 15, 24, 38, 43
barriers to 8–9, 20, 57–58

from corporate food structures 18, 19, 20, 21
    in education 17, 33
Detroit 17–18
DIY: when ordinary people build or repair the things in their daily lives without the
    aid of experts 1
    barriers to 8–9, 20, 57–58
    future of 58–59
    as a social movement 4, 8
DIY coordinators: people who perform DIY behavior in groups or with other
    DIYers in mind 2, 3–4
DIY government 42–51
DIY individualists: people who perform DIY behavior in isolation from others, for
    personal reasons 2–3, 4
DIY lifestylers: people who self-identify as DIYers and center much of their lives
    around DIY action 2, 4, 6, 16, 25
    blogs 52–53
    squatters as 50–51
DIY manuals, first 14
DIY media 51–55
DIY Network 21
Drummond, Ree 52–53

E
Economist 63, 65
Edge, Brian 38
Emerson, Ralph Waldo 2
Engels, Friedrich 11
entrepreneurial DIY: DIY action that people make money from, such as crafting or
    flipping houses 21–25
Etsy 24
Eugene Saturday Market 23–24

F
The Farm, Tennessee 15–16
Ferguson, Sarah 8, 48
Fish, Corina 18
fixer-uppers 21–23
food markets 20
foreclosed homes 48, 49
Fortini, Amanda 64
Foucault, Michel 41–42, 56

Francis, Mark 18
frontier hypothesis 12
future of DIY 58–59

G
gardeners
    backyard 19–20
    community 16–19, 48
    guerrilla 18–19
Gatto, John Taylor 28, 33
Gaviotas 45–46
gentrification 18
geo-caching 40
Gilman Street Project 38, 54
Gintis, Herbert 28
Global South: a term for the less-developed nations of the world, generally in the
    southern hemisphere 10
"God Blessed America" 14
Gottlieb, Lew 15
Gould, Peter 11
government, DIY 42–51
governmentality: Michel Foucault's term for a mindset in which people accept
    external authority unquestioningly 42, 46, 56
Gramsci, Antonio 58
Great Depression 11, 12–14, 46
Greenberg, Edward S. 35
guerrilla gardening 18–19
guidebooks, vacation 39
Guthrie, Woody 13–14

H
Habermas, Jurgen 8
hippies 14–16
The Home Depot 22
home improvement DIYers 21–23
home schooling: teaching one's children at home rather than using the public
    school system 28–33
    transition to public school 31–32
homeless camps 46–48
Homestead Act 1862 12

house-flipping: buying a house, making substantial improvements, then re-selling for a profit 21–23

Houston, Robert 29

I

ideology: the use of ideas to justify action or beliefs 27

Independent Media Center 41

indymedia: a phrase used to describe independent journalists working outside the mainstream, corporate news system 41, 51

itinerant camps 46–48

J

Jenkins, Henry 54

Johnson, Ana Gutierrez 35

Jones, Derek 35

K

Keen, Andrew 53

Kellner, Douglas 54

Kingsolver, Barbara 16

Klein, Joe 13, 14

Klein, Naomi 36

L

lavaca collective 36

Lee, Jenny 8, 18

leisure time 38–40

Lenhart, Amanda 53

Lewis, Avi 36

lifeworld: Jurgen Habermas's term for our personal, emotive, non-public lives (contrast to system) 8

Live Nude Girls Unite! 37

Lowe's 22–23

Lugari, Paolo 45, 46

Lusty Lady strip club 37–38

M

Maker Faire 25

manuals, first DIY 14

Marcuse, Herbert 54

market: part of the capitalist system, where commodities are exchanged for money 3

Ron Mandella Community Garden, Sacramento 18–19
Rosenberg, Scott 52

S
Safe Ground, Sacramento 46, 48
Saturday Market, Eugene 23–24
Seattle protest 1999 41, 51
Sedaris, Amy 25
self-help books 1, 28, 39
self-help groups 5
self-organization 42–51
self-reliance: Ralph Waldo Emerson's term referring to individual control of one's public and private life 2, 25
"shopping our way to safety" 27
The Simple Life 16
Simple Times 25
Smith, Jackie 41
social institutions 5–6
social movements 4, 6, 8, 41
social relationships 7–8, 15
socialization 5
sociological imagination: C. W. Mills' term for understanding personal issues in light of broader social context 10, 57
squat: illegal habitation of a property without the owner's knowledge or permission 4, 17, 48–51
supermarket cooperative 36
system: Jurgen Habermas's term for the public world of work, politics, and the market (contrast to lifeworld) 8
Szasz, Andrew 27

T
The Take 36
"This Land is Your Land" 13
Thomas, Henk 36
Thoreau, Henry David 12
Toma, Eugenia 29
travelers 48–51
Turner, Frederick Jackson 12

U
The Underground Market, San Francisco 20

United Airlines 36
Urban Hive, Sacramento 33–34
urban homesteading 48
U.S. Census Bureau 16, 17, 18, 20

V
vacation guidebooks 39
Van Buskirk, Eliot 53
Varano, Charles 36
Vollmann, William T. 48

W
Waters, Alice 17
Webb, Pamela 12
Weirton Steel Mill, West Virginia 36
Weisman, Alan 45, 46
West, Dawn 41
White, Richard 12
Whyte, William Foote 35, 36
Woofter, T. J. 12
worker cooperative: a worker-owned business that operates in a democratic manner
      for the benefit of all 34–38
working from home 33–34
Worster, Donald 12

Y
Yablonski, Lewis 15
YouTube: a social networking video website where users can post their own content
      53–54

Z
'zines: pamphlets with original content that are handmade and individually distrib-
      uted (contrast to magazines or newspapers) 4, 54
Zinn, Howard 25